San Antonio on Wheels

Lewis Birdsong at the wheel of his Maxwell on Blanco Road, 1910.

San Antonio on Wheels

The Alamo City Learns to Drive

Hugh Hemphill

Foreword by Red McCombs

MAVERICK PUBLISHING COMPANY

MAVERICK PUBLISHING COMPANY
P.O. Box 6355, San Antonio, Texas 78209

Library of Congress Cataloging-in-Publication Data

Hemphill, Hugh, 1953-
    San Antonio on wheels : the Alamo city learns to drive / Hugh Hemphill.
        p. cm.
    Includes bibliographical references and index.
    ISBN 978-1-893271-49-4 (alk. paper)
    1. Transportation—Texas—San Antonio—History. 2. Transportation, Automotive—Texas—San Antonio—
History. 3. Automobiles—Texas—San Antonio—History. I. Title.
    HE310.S25H46 2009
    338.409764'351—dc22

                                                                                                    2009004759

PHOTO CREDITS: Alamo Heights Fire Department 48 (above); ArtPace 63; Bandera Public Library 61 (above); Bank of Texas, Devine 25, 60 (center); Betty and Lewis Birdsong Jr. ii, 6, 8 (above), 9–11, 16, 18–20, 21 (above), 28, 30, 31 (center), 33 (below), 34, 35 (above), 50, 52 (below), 53, 54, 55 (below), 59 (above), 61 (below); Mel Brown Jr. 27; Bryant Browning Monnig and Joan Browning Stratton 22 (below), 31 (top); Hector Cardenas 40, 47; Janice George Clyborne 21 (below), 32, 33 (top), 41, 49 (above); Comfort Heritage Foundation 8 (below), 12–14, 38 (above), 57, 59 (below), 60 (bottom); Howard Darnell 36 (above); Lewis F. Fisher cover, xii, 1, 2, 4, 5, 22 (above), 23, 24, 29 (right), 31 (bottom), 39, 42, 44, 45 (left), 46 (center and bottom), 49 (below), 55 (above), 58, 62 (top); Connie Fulwyler 37 (above); Ed Gaida 43; Joe Herring Jr. 15, 38 (below); E. F. Heydenreich 37 (below); LaVernia Historical Association 3; Red McCombs Automotive Group 64 (above); Dina Rittiman 46 (top); Seguin and Guadalupe County Public Library 26, 36 (below), 48 (below); Texas Department of Transportation 51, 52 (above), 56 (above); Texas Transportation Museum x, 17, 45 (right), 56 (above); Toyota Motor Manufacturing of Texas 64 (below); Uvalde Public Library 60 (top), 62 (above); Pat Wallace 29 (left); Witte Museum 7, 35 (below).

Contents

Foreword

by Red McCombs

Henry Ford once stated that he didn't build the Ford car to take a person from the bank to the post office. His thought was that this car machinery would reduce hard labor and help people be more productive. Did he ever underestimate the human desire to drive oneself wherever and whenever one wanted to go!

History has made clear that the growth and development of civilization is driven by transportation. But the car has always provided more than transportation. It's as much a part of every person's personality as one's dress. As Hugh Hemphill's book demonstrates, San Antonio's history of its love affair with "wheels" is no different than it's been in every other spot on earth.

My father was a country boy, born and raised on a farm. His dream was to someday be able to ride in a car on wheels. He fulfilled that dream at the age of 19, when the Ford dealer in the small Texas town of Spur allowed him to apprentice and develop his skill as an automobile mechanic.

For two years my father's compensation was room and board and tobacco. Well, that's not totally true, because his primary compensation was being able to study the tech manual available at the time on how to repair the Ford car. My father's love for the car was such that he never cared to embrace any other opportunities. He was able to live a life of excitement as he witnessed the advancement of the technology of the automobile.

I guess the apple didn't fall far from the tree, because, as his oldest child, my business career has been built around the sale of automobiles. My car is just as exciting to me today as my Dad's was to him in 1920.

B. J. "Red" McCombs developed San Antonio's oldest Ford company into one of the nation's leading automobile dealerships. He is the namesake of the University of Texas at Austin's McCombs School of Business.

Preface

Folks have only one first car. Like a first love, it will never be forgotten. Ask anyone about his or her first car and you'll be flooded with carefully remembered details. Year, make, model, color, condition, good and bad points, all are stored for a lifetime. You will find out if it was the car one learned to drive in, if it was a gift, if it was new, how long the person owned it. The act of replacement will be tinged with regret, even if it was an old junker.

You might think, therefore, that the first car in San Antonio would be equally well remembered. Its arrival was a momentous occasion, the harbinger of change in the leisurely pace of the city. The arrival of the first train in San Antonio was celebrated for two days, and has never been forgotten. But arrival of the first car was a more private event, not the sudden and dramatic debut of a full-blown transportation system. If chronicled, it was soon forgotten.

I have read entire seven-hundred-page histories of Texas that don't touch on the subject. Some mention when the first train arrived, but, other than that, the epic difficulties of moving people and freight across the vast, often hostile, distances of Texas merit nary a note. Searching for information about Texas in books about national transportation developments is an equally frustrating and ultimately fruitless task.

The arrival of automobiles in the early 1900s brought Texas a new set of opportunities and challenges. A campaign begun by cyclists in the 1890s for better roads in towns and cities expanded into the countryside with autos. Initial resistance of rural communities to better roads faded as opportunities for better access to urban markets for their produce became apparent. Automobiles and better roads relieved the crushing isolation of living on farms and ranches, and access to better paying jobs in cities provided alternatives to back-breaking work on farms and ranches. Attendance at churches soared, as did business at cinemas and other attractions. Going for a pleasure drive on Sundays became a common activity.

My own point of entry in this transportation history is worth mentioning. Within a short time of arriving in Texas from Scotland, I fell in love with a 1958 Imperial at the Texas Transportation Museum. Almost twenty feet long and seven feet wide, swathed in chrome by the square yard and equipped with the truly remarkable 392 Hemi V8 engine, it remains the most American thing I have ever seen. I have been a professional driver on both sides of the Atlantic and have had the opportunity to drive an astonishing array of vehicles, from Ford Model Ts to modern ambulances, but no other country in the world has ever produced such a bold vehicle. Following four years of making the Imperial ready for the road after its long idleness, the car once more took me by surprise by providing the best driving experience of my life.

Under the rear seat I found some original ownership papers that led me to Seguin to find the Pete Smith Plymouth dealership, only to discover that the company had closed its doors thirty years earlier. Thus began my first serious research project. Starting at the local newspaper, I went to the library and from there to Weyel Buick, still located downtown, then on to a local photography store that referred me to the niece of the original owner, who lived in San Antonio. I ended up with more information and pictures than I could possibly have anticipated.

From this experience I learned how willing people are to share their memories and pictures. Folks bring out old scrapbooks that haven't been touched in decades. This willingness aided me in my first book, *The Railroads of San Antonio and South Central Texas*, and now in this one. All thanks to the Imperial—named Mrs. Blueberry by my daughter more than ten years ago.

Hugh Hemphill at the wheel of the 1924 Model T truck he helped restore. Writes the author: "I have never driven a more difficult, noisy and uncomfortable vehicle in my whole life."

While working on this book, as director of the Texas Transportation Museum I had the good fortune to be involved with the restoration of another museum vehicle, a 1924 Ford Model T truck that had not been driven in almost thirty years. The virtues of this iconic vehicle's simplicity and strength soon became apparent. I also had to learn to drive it. This required a different choreography than for modern vehicles. There are three pedals on the floor, but none for the gas. Where you would expect the accelerator is the brake pedal. The speed control is the right hand side lever on the steering column, the spark advance on the left.

I have never driven a more difficult, noisy and uncomfortable vehicle in my life. It gave me a whole new level of respect for the folks who used this crude machine to traverse unpaved roads with tires that required fixing more often than the gas tank needed filling. If the experience hadn't also been extremely enjoyable I probably would not have persevered. I can say the same for this book. Driving the Model T was a good counter balance for hours spent poring through dusty records and blurred microfilms. Both projects yielded far more pleasure than the work required to accomplish them. I hope you find reading this book equally rewarding.

For assistance in writing this book I am particularly grateful to Maverick Publishing's Lewis F. Fisher for his editing assistance and to the following:

In San Antonio, to the Alamo A's, Alamo Area Council of Governments, Alamo Heights Fire Department, Daisy Tours, University of the Incarnate Word archives, Jordan Ford, San Antonio Conservation Society, Mopar Muscle Club, Old Spanish Trail

Association, Red McCombs Automotive Group, San Antonio Transportation Association, San Antonio Wheelmen, T Fords of Texas, SMT Truck Lines, Texas Transportation Museum, Toyota, VIA Metropolitan Transit and the Witte Museum.

To these entitites in other cities: Austin, Texas Department of Transportation; Bandera, Frontier Times Museum; Comfort, Heritage Foundation; Devine, Bank of America; Kerrville, Kerr Regional History Center and Archives; LaVernia, Historical Association; Pleasanton, Longhorn Museum; Rosanky, Central Texas Museum of Automotive History; Seguin, Seguin Heritage Museum; Wichita Falls, Museum of North Texas History and Wichita County Archives; and to public libraries in Bandera, Comfort, Jourdanton, Kerrville, Poteet, San Antonio, Seguin, Uvalde and Wichita Falls.

Also to these individuals: Paula Allen, Chuck Anderson, Ben Bennett, Betty and Lewis Birdsong Jr., Fred Bock, Daniel Bratcher, Hector Cardenas, Don Clark, Anne Cook, Andrew Crews, Virgil Culpepper, Jared Davis, Mike De La Garza, Pat Driscoll, Sister Francisca Eiken, Frank Faulkner, Curtis Foester, Amy Fulkerson, Richard Goeth, Ed Gaida, Pam Gilbert, Roy Gilbert, Jackie Gross, Pat Halpin, Michelle Hammond, Joe Herring Jr., E. F. Heydeneich, William Hudson, Burma Hyde, Charlotte Kahl, Mike Mackechney, Red McCombs, Al McGraw, Pat Monfrey, Lucille Winerich Pipes, Tony Planas, Valerie Purgason, Donna Rice, Dina Rittiman, Andy Scheidt, Marsha Shields, Beth Standifird, Elaine Stephens, Suzy Thomas, Bill Todt, Ralph Wilhelms, Gay Woodward and David Zies.

And I am especially grateful to my wife, Therese, whose patience made this book possible, and to my daughter, Jennifer, who made it worthwhile.

Introduction: Horses, Oxen and Mules

Movement of goods and people has always been vital to San Antonio, crossroads that it is on routes between Mexico and the north and between ports on the Gulf of Mexico and California on the east and west. The city's growth has been due in large part to transportation improvements brought about by daring individuals willing to take advantage of new opportunities.

After Texas was annexed by the United States in 1845, the U.S. Army arrived to set up forts on the Texas frontier. With the Army came not only the need for better transportation but also the U.S. Post Office. It created subsidies allowing stagecoach companies to begin and continue operations, and brought federal involvement in establishing and maintaining road systems. Post roads soon became the safest and best maintained roads in the state.

From the earliest days, the ox cart had been the main means of cross-country transportation. The slow, lumbering wagons were ideal for the lawless and primitive landscape. Oxen had certain advantages over horses and mules. They required little in the way of feed, as they could forage for grass at rest stops. They were relatively inexpensive to buy. Harnessing them to the carts was simple, and their docility meant it was unlikely for a driver to lose control of his heavily laden wagon. They had no value to either Indian tribes or gangs of outlaws, so even if robbed the passengers were unlikely to lose their means of progress.

Mules are faster and can carry heavier loads, and in skilled hands can be driven as many as twelve miles a day under good conditions. But they also attracted Indians, who took every opportunity to steal them. Thus it took some time before mules overtook oxen in hauling heavy goods.

Facing Page: San Antonio's Military Plaza was the hub for horsedrawn transportation in South Texas-until arrival of the railroad in the latter 1870s.

Right: Oxen draw wagons down Commerce Street toward Military Plaza in the 1870s.

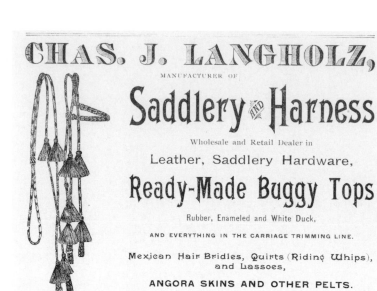

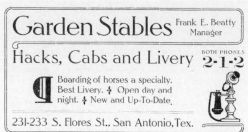

A host of service enterprises thrived on San Antonio's horse-based transportation industry in the nineteenth century.

Coming from a female horse and a male donkey, the mule is somewhere in between in size. With short legs and small, hard, hooves, the animal takes after the donkey in sure-footedness and patience. The mule lacks the free-spirited nature of the horse and, as a creature of habit, is more trainable and docile—so much so that many caporals, the person in charge of the animals on wagon trains, had only to crack their whip first thing in the morning for the mules to obediently arrange themselves not only in front of their own wagon but also precisely within their assigned team arrangement.

Also, a mule's skin is more resistant to the chafing of heavy loads and most forms of weather, though while they can tolerate the sun, their coats—unlike those of horses—are not waterproof, so mules need shelter during heavy rain.

The key date in the history of transportation development in San Antonio is 1845, when Texas became part of the United

Charles Settles and Faustino Ruiz and their horse pause in front of LaVernia's Lay Hotel in 1911.

States. This brought in military units to set up forts west of San Antonio, an influx of immigrants and the U.S. Mail to keep everyone in touch. Mud wagons—the correct name for stagecoaches in Texas—were subsidized by the post office, and were much better than walking.

As mail subsidies made stagecoach service inland from Gulf seaports viable, the first service from Galveston to San Antonio and Austin began twice a week in 1847. Both people and freight were transported in mule-driven wagons sturdier than the classic later Wells-Fargo stagecoaches. Stops were approximately every twelve miles, which could take up to four hours of travel. At each stop the exhausted mules were exchanged and weary passengers got a chance to stretch their legs.

With the end of the Mexican War in 1848, San Antonio leaders financed an expedition of thirty-seven Texas Rangers to establish a route west to El Paso. The group managed to get as far as Presidio before turning back. Discovery of gold in California soon made such a route even more essential, since the shortest cross-country route to California for miners arriving at ports on the Gulf of Mexico was across Texas.

Subsequent expeditions established two routes to El Paso, a lower route, via Del Rio—essentially the course of today's Highway 90—and an upper route—the basic path of today's IH 10—which avoided the Pecos Mountains, and, though longer, was considered easier for wagon trains and faster for stagecoaches.

Blacksmithing remained the main business at the Tobin Hill Blacksmith Shop north of downtown San Antonio, though by 1920 accomodations were being made for automobile work.

In the late 1850s, several new San Antonio stagecoach services emerged. One went to Corpus Christi twice a week and to Laredo, via Pleasanton, once a week. Another weekly line traveled between San Antonio and Fredericksburg, via Bandera and Kerrville. One could travel more directly to Fredericksburg via Boerne and Comfort on the main stagecoach route to El Paso.

Arrival of the railroad from Houston in 1877 changed the nature of transportation services. Trips that once took days suddenly took only hours. But the flood of new immigrants into San Antonio and deep into the surrounding territory not accessible by rail still needed transportation, and the increasing numbers of passengers allowed more frequent service. Increasing prosperity allowed people to buy fancy traps and surreys for going to church and social occasions.

By the 1870s San Antonio had three carriage and wagon making businesses—Danenhauer & Seffel, M. Eckenroth and Louis Vollrath. Ancillary enterprises included harness makers, livestock dealers, horse traders and tanneries that rendered carcasses into hides.

When the first gasoline-powered horseless carriage arrived in San Antonio in 1901, there were sixty-five blacksmiths listed in the city directory along with three carriage painters and trimmers and four wagon makers and vendors: C. H. Dean on South Flores Street, August Staacke on Commerce Street, D. J. Woodward on Main Avenue and a newcomer, Brown, Sloan & Alexander on Dolorosa Street, taking the place of an older firm, R. H. Hofheinz, in business on Avenue D for more than a decade. There were also ten livery stables and nine harness and saddle outlets.

At the San Antonio International Fair in 1902, Staacke Brothers—San Antonio's foremost livery service—was demonstrating electric vehicles built by Studebaker, and the Roach & Barnes bicycle store was showing steam-powered vehicles built by Locomobile.

As late as the 1940s, C. H. Gurinsky was still able to keep his focus on selling horses and mules to South Texas ranchers.

Even in 1910, as the number of automobile sales outlets jumped to nineteen, there were still three companies building wagons—C. Gersdorf on Zavala Street, P. Schiffer & Son on Austin Street and S. Seffel & Sons on East Crockett Street—plus eight carriage and wagon outlets and eleven livery establishments. In that year, city council issued the first set of road rules taking motorized vehicles into consideration.

Among other requirements, drivers of horseless carriages were obliged to bring their vehicles to a complete stop at the bidding of a horse rider or wagon driver. By 1921, this obligation had been removed. Horses were little mentioned, except that leaving horse-drawn wagons unattended was not permitted. Nor were automobile drivers allowed to deliberately scare horses.

Horses and mules drawing buckboards, carriages and wagons remained vital to everyday life until after World War I, when the burden was finally lifted off the back of man's most loyal servants with the full arrival of the automobile age.

1. Bicycles, Velocipedes and High-Wheelers

On May 6, 1869, the San Antonio *Herald* ran a piece about a local man named Muhl who had built a velocipede, a two-wheeled machine built before the introduction of safety bicycles. It is the first published mention of a bicycle in San Antonio. "Who," the writer asked, "will hereafter say that San Antonio is not a fast place?"

Muhl's velocipede was no doubt a "boneshaker," with wooden wheels, metal rims and pedals directly attached to the front wheels. Parts were readily available by mail. On the same page appeared an advertisement for velocipede wheels made in Dayton, Ohio.

The first American bicycle club—the League of American Wheelmen—was started during the high-wheeler era in 1880. These machines had one very high wheel and another much smaller one. A rudimentary form of mechanical advantage that allowed for greater speed came with front wheels often five feet in diameter, and the distance traveled by the wheel for one revolution of the pedals was huge. The disadvantage was that the rider was prone to flipping over the top of the wheel if it met an obstruction, leading to the phrase "breakneck speed." There were no gears, and the brakes were largely ineffective.

San Antonio's first bicycle store opened in the early 1880s, at 302 West Commerce Street. It was owned by Jacob France and August Thiele and sold high-wheelers.

Facing Page: Emerson & Crothers partners selling and repairing bicycles on East Houston Street in 1898 were Frank Crothers, left, and Ed Emerson.

Right: With their high-wheelers in 1878 were, from left, Albert Steves, Gus Kampmann and Edward Steves Jr.

Youngsters could manage three wheels while their
elders, top, cycled individually on two-wheelers or as
a couple on tandems, the lady riding in front where
a low crossbar made room for her skirt.

The Bicycle Craze

The first modern bicycles, similar to those still in use, were introduced in England in 1879 and first manufactured in appreciable numbers in France. The new machines were called safety bicycles, as they resolved most of the dangers and difficulties encountered on previous attempts at traveling on two wheels. Unlike its predecessors, the safety bicycle achieved strength and speed by using a lightweight tubular frame and smaller, geared wheels of the same size, enabling riders to achieve and maintain considerable speeed and making ascending hills an easier proposition.

With the smaller wheels and location of the pedals within the frame directly under the rider, the new machines had a much lower center of gravity, which meant falling off was less likely and less dangerous. The safety bicycle had effective brakes that made avoiding obstacles and other road users easier. A chain-driven rear wheel allowed the rider to stop pedaling even if the rear wheel was turning, a significant improvement over the direct-drive bone-shakers of the past.

The safety bicycle arrived as an expensive import to America in 1886. Two years later Alexander Pope in Boston designed the Columbia, built by a sewing machine company, and became the father of the American safety bicycle. Introduction of air-filled tires enabled both greater speeds and a higher degree of comfort. Almost immediately the improved safety bicycle became the wonder of the world. Acetylene lamps enabled evening and night time riding. By 1897 more than three hundred companies were making more than a million machines a year, and nearly half the designs submitted to the U.S. Patent Office pertained to bicycles.

At the Roach & Barnes bicycle shop on West Comerce Street, Claude Mills is behind the counter in 1898, top, across from Lewis Birdsong; below, Birdsong, left, and Jim Roach inspect the inventory of inner tubes for bicycle tires.

Manufacture of the safety bicycle signified the beginning of the modern era of individual transportation. The machines accelerated development of such familiar items as ball bearings, tubular construction, air-filled rubber tires and wire-spoked wheels. They were one of the first mass-produced items designed for everyday use, bringing the cost down to an affordable level. Although bicycles were soon eclipsed by automobiles, for a brief time they captured the imagination of people hungry for new experiences and better ways of doing things. They were relatively inexpensive to buy and even cheaper to operate. They enabled people to travel far beyond walking distance without much additional effort while avoiding the work involved in using horses and mules.

The first bicycle club in San Antonio was formed in 1891—the Alamo Wheelmen, a chapter of the League of American Wheelmen. C. R. Clifford was president and George Walker vice-president. These gentlemen were the first in the area to promote the exciting new machines. For four years the club's racing team was comprised of Sam Lawyer, Harry W. Hale and J. A. Roach, who participated in bicycle racing events throughout the state. Roach

West Houston Street's Texas Cycle Works, shown in 1896, specialized in the sale of Munger bicycles.

was also a member of the family that co-owned the largest bicycle emporium in town in the late 1890s, Roach & Barnes, at 307 West Commerce Street. Co-owner W. E. Roach was a frequent referee at local bicycle races.

At 129 West Commerce Street, Wagner & Chabot were advertising the new top-of-the-line Columbia for $80—today's equivalent of $2,000—and a used one for $60. A mid-range Sterling was $65 ($45 used), and a lower-range Hartford was $50. Still operating was the pioneering shop of Jacob France and August Thiele, who claimed to have introduced pneumatic tires to the city and who also fabricated an innovative but somewhat cumbersome outrigger system that allowed novices to get the experience of being on two wheels before they learned how to ride the tricky new machines.

Bicycles could also be purchased from H. Rhein at 601 Austin Street, R. H. "Hugo" Hofheinz at 111 Avenue D—where free riding lessons were available prior to purchase—and from the Texas Cycle Works at 117 West Houston Street, which specialized in Munger bicycles and had several employees who did repairs as well. Department stores such as Joske's sold them, as did Schreiner's in Kerrville. In smaller towns bicycles were often available from agricultural supply stores or even blacksmith shops.

In 1898, two brothers-in-law at different bicycle shops teamed up to open their own: W. Frank Crothers, who worked for Texas Cycle Works, and Lewis F. Birdsong, an employee of Roach & Barnes.

Crothers & Birdsong opened in a small space at 214 ½ West Houston Street, ultimately the site of the Majestic Theater. They at first sold only the National, a racing bicycle noted for its light weight. The National, intended only for those in serious competition, was expensive, so to supplement their revenue the partners repaired bicycles and typewriters and became a Kodak agency for cameras, film and photo processing.

Roach & Barnes helped keep its early competitive edge by promoting itself in this float in an early Fiesta parade, in 1896.

Frank Crothers rounds a turn on the banked oval of boards built in the 1890s to accommodate bikers around the perimeter of the San Antonio Jockey Club's horse racing track, off Broadway near present-day Lion's Field.

The Bicycle Racing Circuit

Crothers and Birdsong joined three others—L. J. Scheutze, C. J. Scheidemantel and C. A. Baker—on a team known as the Independent Five, which competed on the Texas bicycle racing circuit. The Independent Five's motto was "Keep In Front." Their Nationals, stripped of such extraneous equipment as brakes and gears, weighed less than thirteen pounds, and could be packed flat into narrow canvas carrying cases for easy railroad baggage transportation. Nationals were a fixed-wheel bicycle—a type still in use—featuring rear wheels that turned when the pedals were moving, without any free-wheeling mechanism to save weight. Such machines need skilled riders but can achieve high speed on high-banked oval, quarter-mile wooden race tracks. Without brakes, the rider can stop by reducing pedaling and applying back pressure or by leaning forward and applying leather-gloved hands to the front tire.

San Antonio, Laredo and Galveston were soon joined by Houston and Dallas on the Texas bicycle racing circuit of the 1890s, as bicycle racing became the top spectator sport in the nation. Riders such as Marshall "Major" Taylor, the black cyclist who overcame initial exclusion to become the undisputed world bicycling champion, were national heroes. Racers from throughout the country competed against those from Texas; many of its towns had at least one professional rider. Cuero had George Anderson, Corpus Christi had J. F. McCann, Bastrop had Bruno Elzner and Waco had L. W. Johnson.

The pride of San Antonio was longtime Alamo Wheelman member and dealer R. H. Hofheinz, who also organized road races. In 1896 Crothers and Birdsong took part in one of Hofheinz's races over the "Mission Course." Five hundred people on foot and in carriages gathered at the starting and finish point at the intersection of Roosevelt Avenue and Perieda Street. Many more lined the unpaved streets to witness the excitement. The winner took just over forty minutes to negotiate the course of some fifteen miles, and the last of the thirteen riders took just over fifty minutes. Crothers came in third and Birdsong ninth.

In the late 1890s, both Houston and Dallas built bicycle racing velodromes that could seat upwards of two thousand people around high-banked, quarter mile ovals of wooden boards. San Antonio did not have such a venue dedicated solely to bicycle racing. Instead, a high-banked board oval was built around the dirt horse racing track belonging to the San Antonio Jockey Club, just off Broadway north of downtown near the present site of Lion's Field. To accommodate race-day crowds, additional streetcars were run to the site.

An event on June 5, 1896, was part of the national circuit and attracted many professional riders who had participated in races in Phoenix, Arizona, two days earlier. Amateur races filled up the card, and once again Lewis Birdsong was in the thick of things. He placed first in the one-mile novice race, in two minutes twenty-five seconds; third in the half-mile amateur race, at one minute eight seconds; and second in the one-mile amateur race, at two minutes twenty seconds.

In his first race in 1896, Birdsong won a diamond stud value at $25 for his first place in the one-mile novice race, plus a diamond pin worth $20 for a second place and a bicycle saddle worth $5 for a third place. His other prizes over a two-year period ranged from a camera in another San Antonio race, a pair of opera glasses in Waco and a sweater for a second place in Taylor.

These ladies rode decorated bicycles to a picnic in Comfort in 1913.

Two couples on early motorcycles beside the Guadalupe River in Comfort in 1913.

Rules for Riding

For women, bicycles with lower crossbars were introduced to accommodate bulky petticoats and skirts. Although bicycles were hailed as particularly liberating for women, proper standards still had to be maintained. In 1895, the San Antonio *Express* detailed the etiquette of bicycle riding. The correct phrase was "cycling," not "bicycling" and certainly not "wheeling." There were specific rules for getting on and off bicycles. A gentleman should not stand astride the machine during a conversation. He should be prepared to extend any and all courtesies to members of the fairer sex, including dismounting first to steady the lady's bicycle and holding it once more as she got on. He was expected to be capable of making all repairs, lest the lady's white gloves become besmirched with oil and grime.

A woman riding alone was absolutely beyond the pale. A gentleman escort, riding to the left, was preferred—such as a husband or brother—but a maid would do if no suitable man was available. No decent lady was to be seen on a bicycle after midday, unless attending a bicycle tea or a related social event.

All bicycles were to be equipped with a clock, luggage carrier, cyclometer and a bell—the latter a legal requirement, since city rules adopted in 1898 required a cyclist to ring his or her bell three times within fifteen feet of a street crossing. A speed limit of eight miles per hour was imposed within city limits. A furor erupted within the council when the speed limit was increased a few years later, leading to the abrupt resignation of at least one representative.

Arrival of the first automobiles in San Antonio soon diminished the city's fascination with the bicycle, as happened in cit-

Postmaster Adolph Kutzer rode his Harley-Davidson to deliver rural mail near Comfort in 1913.

ies throughout the nation. The bicycle craze receded and prices dropped, and the machines became simply a low-cost form of transportation and recreation. As the industry consolidated, the space devoted to bicycles in the 1900 Sears catalog dropped to three pages, half the number of three years before, while the prices of the machines fell even further. A top-of-the-line Acme King, available for both men and women, cost only $15.75, a far cry from the $56.50 needed to acquire the 1897 premium model. The mid-range Acme Prince could be had for $14.75 and the Acme Jewel for $13.75.

As bicycles blended into the background, bicycle races throughout the state faded away. The last at the San Antonio Jockey Club track were held in 1910. Still, in 1911, before many homes had telephones, San Antonio's city directory listed five bicycle messenger services.

In outlying areas of San Antonio, where roads hardly existed, individuals and even whole clubs installed outriggers on their bicycles so they could use them on railroad tracks and bridges. This was quite safe, as the Artesian Belt Railroad, for one, ran only one train a day in each direction six days a week, leaving the tracks mostly free for other users.

Motorcycles

Climbing hills and dealing with faster, heavier road vehicles made the work of riding a bicycle on a regular basis over long distances both hard work and hazardous. Installing gasoline engines on bicycles had to wait until the earliest engines were lightweight enough. The first motorcycles produced commercially in the United States were the Orients built by the Metz Company

This messenger used an early motorcycle to deliver telegrams in Kerrville.

of Waltham, Massachusetts, using French-built DeDion motors. In 1903 Lewis Birdsong raced an Orient in one of the first Texas motorcycle races, held in Houston.

The first all-American motorcycles—Indians—were first made in 1901 in Springfield, Massachusetts, by a professional bicycle rider and manufacturer, George Hendee, and an engineer, Carl Hedstorm. Two years later, boyhood friends William Harley and Arthur Davidson introduced theirs in Milwaukee, Wisconsin.

Until World War I, Indian was the world's largest motorcycle manufacturer. Motorbikes were less expensive than automobiles but less practical, having almost no load-carrying capacity. The addition of a sidecar added the ability to carry a second passenger, but sidecars were never really popular. Motorcycles were, however, quickly adopted by law enforcement agencies. The San Antonio Police Department purchased its first in 1910, the same year it acquired its first automobiles. In 1919, Comal County hired motorcycle cops to ticket motorists who ignored the eighteen-mile-an-hour speed limit. Motorcycles were also used for carrying the relatively light loads of mail over rural routes.

Mr. and Mrs. R. G. Thomas in their Maxwell Runabout on College Street in 1908.

2. The Horseless Carriage Comes to San Antonio

One of the most memorable pieces of music dealing with the automobile was written to promote Oldsmobile's Curved Dash model, the nation's first mass-produced automobile.

Frank and Charles Duryea built America's first internal combustion vehicle in 1893 in Springfield, Massachusetts. Two years later they took part in the first automobile race, organized by a Chicago newspaper. Held in December, conditions over the fifty-four mile course of unimproved public roads were atrocious, and only the Duryea managed to complete the race. But the Duryeas failed to capitalize on their front-runner status and were soon left behind by more enterprising individuals such as Alexander Pope, who had created the earlier bicycle boom.

At first, each horseless carriage was hand crafted and unique. Following traditions of carriage making, it used a lot of wood. Standardization of measurements had yet to be achieved, so parts were hand worked to make them fit together. With such low production, each vehicle expanded the builder's knowledge of what did and didn't work, aided by such trade publications as *The American Machinist*, which first published articles on "How To Build An Automobile" in 1895. Almost all manufacturers were self-taught. Henry Ford and David Buick had backgrounds in engineering and metal work, but few had any college education.

Ransom Olds established what became America's first significant car company, Oldsmobile, in 1897. Using a rudimentary form of production line assembly, in 1901 Olds built some 400 simple and lightweight "runabouts" with a curved dashboard of the type found at the front of horse-drawn carriages to protect the occupants from dust and other debris. The following year the number rose to 2,500, and the vehicle, by now known as the "Curved Dash" for its signature design element, became an icon of the modern age. In 1903, one of his cars was driven from New York to the Pacific, the first to make the trip from east to west.

At the first automobile show at New York's Madison Square Garden in October 1900, thirty-four cars were displayed. Nineteen were powered by gasoline, seven by steam, six by batteries. There were two gasoline electric hybrids. By 1908, cars were shown by more than one hundred different manufacturers. Automobile advertisements were appearing in the *Saturday Evening Post* and automobile magazines were on the newsstands: *Horseless Age, Motorcycle & Automobile Maker & Dealer, Motor and Automobile Topics*. But the cars were relatively expensive, and there was no financing. A Ford Model C cost $950 and a Maxwell was $1,400, today's equivalent of $31,900.

The First Horseless Carriages in San Antonio

The first horseless carriage on the streets of San Antonio was most likely an electric vehicle built in 1897 for Montgomery Ward, America's first catalog company. Montgomery Ward took several of these technological marvels on promotional tours around Texas that year. San Antonio, the largest city in the state, would have been a logical destination, though confirmation of such a visit has yet to be found.

In August 1899 the San Antonio *Express* announced "The Automobile is Coming" when one or two electrics were to be on display at the San Antonio International Fair. The first recorded horseless carriage in the city was delivered that October to the Staacke Brothers carriage dealership. Though its manufacturer was not named, the electric was described as a one-seat road wagon, light in appearance and with wooden wheels and rubber tires. A description of its performance had to wait, however, as it was delivered without batteries.

Also in 1899 a prototype steam-powered vehicle built in San Antonio the previous year by George H. Lutz. The Lutz Steam Company did not survive the year, though eighteen years later Lutz re-emerged as head of the Lutz Motor Car Company, a manufacturer of steam cars in Buffalo, New York. One of its four directors was a probable relative, Orman Lutz of San Antonio.

The first gasoline horseless carriage in Texas is commonly credited to a machine built by the St. Louis Automobile Company and purchased by Edward Green of Terrell in 1899. The first gasoline-powered car in San Antonio was a Haynes-Apperson, brought to the city in 1901 by J. D. Anderson, cashier at City National Bank. It cost $1,795, today's equivalent of $45,000. Not everyone was excited about Anderson's purchase. A group of citizens unsuccessfully petitioned city hall to enact an ordinance forbidding the use of such dangerous contraptions.

This trio was enjoying an outing in 1904 in their Curved Dash Oldsmobile, the type that Frank Crothers and Lewis Birdsong had sent to San Antonio by train and assembled in Birdsong's back yard two years earlier.

After selling Oldsmobiles, Lewis Birdsong became a dealer in Maxwells, including this 1910 Sports Roadster he took a turn in.

At that time Lewis F. Birdsong and W. Frank Crothers owned a small bicycle, Kodak and typewriter repair shop at 214 East Houston Street in the heart of downtown San Antonio. In the summer of 1902, without fanfare, they added horseless carriages to their product line and became the city's first automobile agency. They ordered a $650 gasoline-powered Curved Dash Oldsmobile, the nation's first mass-produced car. It was crated by the manufacturer, sent by train to San Antonio and delivered by a horse-drawn wagon to Birdsong's backyard at 708 Marshall Street.

Oldsmobile would have provided a mechanic to help put the vehicle together and provide driving lessons, but Crothers and Birdsong, though they had never actually seen a gasoline-powered vehicle, decided to do it themselves.

Birdsong wrote that it did not take long to assemble the lightweight vehicle. The one-cylinder engine was attached under the seat, and the tiller steering apparatus was installed in the center of the curved dashboard. There were three gears, two forward and reverse, with brakes operating on both the differential and the rear wheels. The twenty-eight-inch wooden wheels had wooden spokes and pneumatic tires. After adding oil, filling the five-gallon fuel tank and cranking the engine, the Oldsmobile sputtered to life.

After driving their vehicle backward and forward in the yard, the two took it out onto the unpaved streets, where the highly articulated wheels dealt with ruts and bumps with relative ease and allowed speeds of up to twelve miles per hour. Next the pair took the Oldsmobile out to the race track at the International Fair-

Welcome Smith pauses at Seguin during a 1904 tour in which this Oldsmobile became the first automobile seen in many Texas communities.

The only virtue of the low-cost Brush, with its wooden frame and four-cylinder engine, was that it was cheap. It was introduced in 1910 and is shown in San Antonio two years later, but its manufacture soon ended.

grounds—now Riverside Park—where they reached the dizzying speed of thirty miles per hour.

Birdsong soon had orders for more Curved Dash Oldsmobiles. Buyers included merchant James M. Vance, dentist Frank Barber and San Antonio Drug Company President Fred W. Cook Jr., soon to become president of San Antonio's first automobile club. On September 16, 1902 he sold one to G. E. Vaughn, who tied his trophy deer over the hood and drove home to Alabama.

Two years later Birdsong took his friend Welcome Smith—who would soon manage a taxicab company—on an Oldsmobile promotion drive through Texas, making reports to newspapers as their horseless carriage became the first seen in many of the communities they visited. In 1905 another bicycle shop—Roach & Barnes—became the first to advertise automobiles in the city directory.

At the time Ransom Olds decided to leave his own company in 1905, Birdsong and his new partner, George Potchernick, who also owned a successful camping and sports equipment store, dropped the Oldsmobile and began selling Maxwells, followed by Stoddard-Dayton sports cars and the low-cost Brush, introduced in 1910. That vehicle cost about the same as the Ford Model T, brought to market two years earlier.

Unlike the Ford, the Brush's only virtue was being cheap. It was built almost entirely of wood and had a four-cylinder engine, while the Model T used steel three times stronger than any of its competitors. The Brush failed to catch on and quickly faded away.

Birdsong and Potchernick's fortunes might have been greater had they known that Oldsmobile would become a major part of General Motors, formed in 1908. But Birdsong had become a true believer in the air-cooled Franklin and was not interested in going back. And who could know that General Motors would survive in the face of the ultimate competition, Henry Ford's Model T, introduced the same year.

A 1912 air-cooled Franklin, still with the usual start-up crank in front but with louvered air vents in place of the customary radiator, is driven by San Antonio Franklin dealer Lewis Birdsong on a family outing.

Steamers and Electrics

In January 1902, the steam-powered Locomobile appeared in city streets as Louis Heurmann became Locomobile's San Antonio's individual sales representative. The vehicle was described as "gliding noiselessly over the pavements and under complete control of the occupant," one which "shot forward without any apparent effort, propelled by some aforeseen power." The next month a Locomobile arrived from Bridgeport, Connecticut, at the city's largest bicycle store, Roach & Barnes, on February 2, 1902. For a month the store advertised in the San Antonio *Express* for people to "See the Real Thing" at its 218 West Commerce Street location.

Steam-powered vehicles at first had extremely limited range as, like early steam locomotives, their boilers had to be replenished frequently. When a method to re-circulate the steam was devised along with a faster method to raise pressure, steam-powered vehicles, promoted most strongly by the Stanley Steamer Company, were strong contenders to win the popularity contest against gasoline and electricity and power sources. But steamers had serious drawbacks, in particular their heavy weight and the need to carry water tanks and boilers in addition to the actual engine.

Water to fuel the steamers, however, was easily available, and acquiring quality gasoline was a problem for many years. At first gasoline had to be bought by the bucket from hardware stores and blacksmiths willing to carry the highly flammable fluid. Then it had to be strained through muslin or chamois to remove impurities, especially water. The discovery of plentiful quantities of petroleum near Beaumont, Texas, in 1901 reduced the cost of gasoline. As the gradual development of filling stations improved the supply, steamers were eclipsed, though they lingered into the 1920s.

Electrics had an initial surge of popularity. Of the 8,000 horseless carriages in America in 1900, more than half were elec-

Henry Ford's Model T, first manufactured in 1908, became the ultimate competitor for the myriad of automobile brands then on the market. This Model T is parked at the home of early San Antonio Ford dealer Clifton George.

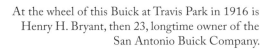

Women found compact electric cars easy to start. This decorated electric was a prizewinner in the Fiesta Battle of Flowers Fiesta parade in 1913.

trics. The biggest manufacturer was Alexander Pope, father of the American bicycle, who sold more than 4,000 Columbia electrics, including taxis, ambulances and delivery vehicles. Electrics were hailed as a huge improvement in public health: no more mountains of manure and dead animals to dispose of daily, and so quiet, too. In October 1902, Staacke Brothers, the city's largest livery service provider and carriage and wagon dealer, which also marketed Studebaker carriages, invited people to its exhibit areas at the San Antonio International Fair to take a ride in the new Studebaker Electric Automobile, and to place orders.

The most important advantage of electrics was that they were easy to start, and thus were particularly popular with women. In San Antonio, Judge T. T. Vanderhoeven bought a 1906 Woods Electric Victoria for his wife, Eva. On her first attempt to drive it, her car caught a man's coat and ended up dragging him the length of Alamo Plaza. The case was settled with the purchase of a new suit of clothes for the victim. However, Mrs. Vanderhoeven refused to drive the vehicle again. It was stored in the garage—untouched—for many years until it was donated to San Antonio's Witte Museum, which still owns it.

Although fairly simple to maintain and operate, electric cars were hindered by the limited range of their heavy batteries and the

At the wheel of this Buick at Travis Park in 1916 is Henry H. Bryant, then 23, longtime owner of the San Antonio Buick Company.

An effort to smooth Fort Sam Houston's roads and reduce dust through a Magnolia Petroleun Company process was unsuccessful.

WIDENING COMMERCE STREET
ALAMO NATIONAL BANK BUILDING
ON ITS JOURNEY OF 16FEET-7 INCHES

To widen Commerce Street for the increasing volume of automobile traffic, the new Alamo National Bank building was rolled back from its initial site.

length of time it took to re-charge them. Their advantage of being easier to start than hand-cranked gasoline-powered cars ended after a friend of Cadillac founder Henry Leland died of gangrene that set in after his arm was broken trying to start a gasoline-powered car. In one of the ironies of history, the introduction of the electric starter in 1911 led to the rapid decline of battery-powered cars.

New Streets, and Rules for Driving

In 1898 Market Street in San Antonio was one of the first streets in Texas to be given a top layer of natural asphalt, from the only limestone asphalt mine in Texas, near Uvalde, which operated until 1935. It was crudely applied by Parker-Washington contractors for several blocks on either side of the intersection with St. Mary's Street. The surface stayed smooth and impervious until 1910, when it was replaced during a $220,000 street widening.

A less than successful method to smooth roads and reduce dust was tried at Fort Sam Houston in 1910 by Dallas-based Magnolia Petroleum Company, which promised the Army: "Magnolia Road Oil, properly applied by Magnolia Modern Methods, solves the dust problem by preventing the formation of 95 percent of the dust."

The post's dirt roads were dragged and rolled, then sprayed with oil. The result was described as disagreeable for the first few days, and the long-term results were not much better. New ruts formed quickly. The oil remained gooey, especially in the heat of the day. It stuck to tires and undercarriages, not to mention the boots of marching soldiers. Similar attempts were made elsewhere with similar results.

San Antonio's streets, dating from Spanish times, quickly proved too narrow for passing automobiles. The face of the city changed as major downtown streets were widened by removing buildings or facades along one side. Widening of Soledad Street to the east in 1910 caused the loss of the Veramendi Palace, the state's finest residence remaining from Spanish times. Widening of Market Street to the north in the mid-1920s cost the city its

As automobiles captured the public imagination, those without wheels could appear to be up to date by having their photograph taken at "Automobile Station," a faux setting in the Smith Studios concession at Electric Park, near San Pedro Park.

Auto repair shops springing up were aided by development of spare parts distribution systems. like that of Long Ford Auto Parts.

historic 1869 Market House, even as protestors joined to form the San Antonio Conservation Society.

The city's largest street widening project of the era was that of Commerce Street, the main artery through the center of the city, in 1913–15. One building saved along the south side of the street was the new five-story Alamo National Bank building, raised onto rollers and moved back while business continued inside.

As more cars traveled along widened streets, safety became a problem. "Automobile Runs Wild" was a San Antonio headline in 1904 for a story describing collision of a car carrying convention delegates with another auto, which remained sufficiently mobile to pick up occupants of the demolished car and take them to their destination. The same year James W. Collins, superintendent of the automobile division of Staacke Brothers, was in a runabout with a prospective customer when their car collided with a streetcar. "The running gear was badly buckled, the wooden body of the vehicle twisted and broken and the engine disarranged" in the wreck. Collins "suffered painfully," but the customer escaped injury.

The city's first automobile-related fatality came in November 1907, when Benice Lecompte, 11, was struck at the corner of San Pedro Avenue and Elmira Street.

A New Year's Eve incident in which a driver sped around a downtown corner at eight miles and hour "and came very near killing several people" provoked Alderman Arthur I. Lockwood into proposing a "rather rigid" ordinance regulating automobiles and their drivers. A full set of formal road municipal rules for the automobile was passed by the city council in March 1910.

As it had been left to local jurisdictions to determine on which side of the road to drive, the San Antonio council ruled that "vehicles going in opposite directions shall pass each other on the right," a tradition that had begun with stagecoaches to make it easier to transfer mail to and from the passing wagons. Until introduction of the Ford Model T in 1908, most cars had the driver on the right, even though they were also almost always driven on

In about 1912 filling stations began installing underground gasoline tanks, safer and less likely to form condensation that mixed water with fuel.

the right side of the road. The Model T's more convenient left-hand drive position was a major hook for would-be buyers.

The new city regulations, published in booklet form, contained detailed instructions and diagrams about how vehicles were to make right and left turns. One could not park with the left side of the car against the curb. Driving on sidewalks was forbidden. The speed limit was eight miles per hour within one mile of San Fernando Cathedral and fifteen miles per hour beyond that. Three driving violations would lead to permanent loss of the driving permit. Entering a vehicle not your own without the permission of the driver or owner was deemed unlawful. A medical exam was required before a permit would be issued.

All vehicles, including horse-drawn wagons, were to be registered at city hall. The fee of two dollars included a license tag composed of letters no smaller than six inches in height to be attached to the rear of the vehicle in such a way that light from the rear marker would illuminate it at night.

Even as late as 1910, horses had priority within San Antonio. Upon request or a signal by a person riding a horse or driving a wagon, an automobile driver was to swiftly come to a stop until the animals had passed. The rules did not require the engine to be switched off, perhaps a concession to the difficulty of starting engines.

Filling Up

Finding a gasoline station in the infancy of the automobile age required locating a livery stable, blacksmith or hardware store that carried the highly combustible fluid. If you were lucky, it would come in one gallon cans, the kind also used for motor oil. More than likely, however, the fuel was stored outdoors in a large raised tank made of wood or metal, and you needed your own bucket to transport the gasoline to your vehicle, where the tank was often under the driver's seat, not easy to access. As storage tanks cooled at night condensation formed inside, and the emptier tanks became, the worse the problem of water mixing with the gasoline. To avoid getting water, as well as rust and other debris, into your tank, it was advisable to strain the fuel through a chamois.

The first fuel pumps were located on the edge of the sidewalk. It was quickly realized that this was quite dangerous, as one bad move by a driver could bring catastrophe. Thus modern filling stations began to emerge around 1912. They were characterized by pumps on raised islands in the middle of a forecourt well off the main roadway and had underground tanks to hold the fuel, which was safer and reduced condensation. The customer or an employee hand-pumped fuel into a sight glass at the top of the pump. This allowed the customer to see exactly how much gas he or she was getting before gravity drained it into the vehicle's tank.

The development of a network of filling stations took several decades. It was advisable to carry extra fuel as well as tires, which were highly prone to failure for a similar period of time. Most early dealerships sold both, and often made more revenue from servicing cars than they did from vehicle sales.

The cost of gasoline doubled from 15 to 30 cents a gallon in 1920, when nearly half the gas being sold was from filling stations. A decade later it was more than 90 percent. Filling stations had become service stations, as they were also selling parts, tires, replacing glass and performing repairs. In San Antonio they were often called ice houses, as long-established corner stores added this service to their sales of ice, bread, dairy products and beer. Some became community centers, with parties complete with dances and bands playing on the roof in the evening.

Also more common in San Antonio than elsewhere were multi-story structures that allowed cars to fill up on the ground level while floors above were rented as offices. These were located on busy downtown corners to allow drivers access from two streets.

While many service stations were independently owned, most were allied to one of the major fuel suppliers. Within San Antonio

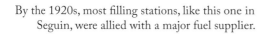
By the 1920s, most filling stations, like this one in Seguin, were allied with a major fuel supplier.

Staton Brown's Service Station at 218 South New Braunfels Avenue had a white tank for "white," or unleaded, gas.

the dominant oil companies until 1920 were Gulf Oil, now part of Chevron; Magnolia, which provided the Pegasus symbol to its successor, Mobil; and the Texas Company, which became Texaco. Each developed distinctive designs. Gulf, which began processing Spindletop oil in 1901, first used hexagonal boxes with overhanging canopies at the center of their stations. Magnolia featured a small hut with a large continuous canopy. The Texas Company used a dog-run style with continuous roof over two separate rooms and a space between for cars to drive through to access the pumps.

These companies were joined by Cities Service, with its mission-inspired Spanish Eclectic style with tile roofs and raised brick pilasters at each corner of the main building and unshaded pumps in the forecourt. Humble Oil, now part of Exxon, used a house with canopy design, with brick veneers and supporting columns. Sinclair favored ornate structures, some with two canopies, with stucco exterior walls, distinctive gables and pent roof parapets covered with green tile.

Since zoning laws were initially viewed as unconstitutional restrictions upon the rights of property owners, many early gas stations were located in the heart of residential districts, then grandfathered when zoning was enacted.

Neighborhoods gained other auto-related amenities. In 1929 the Rapid Auto Laundry opened on North Main Avenue at Richmond and Elmira streets. There a car could be washed, polished and vacuumed in two minutes. The plant's capacity was 250 vehicles per day.

3. Selling, Racing and Building Autos

Standard references do not always reflect what was really happening, literally, on the streets. City directories make no mentions of car dealers in San Antonio until 1909, when two businesses were listed as selling automobiles, though dealers had been selling cars in the city as early as 1902.

When in 1907 it became state law to register automobiles, some 20,000 vehicles were recorded in Texas. Easily a thousand or more would have been in San Antonio, and their numbers were growing quickly.

Indeed, in San Antonio's 1910 city directory the number of automobiles dealers jumped to nineteen. The next year there were twenty-five, plus a variety of auto-related companies—sixteen repair shops, eight automobile rental companies, six parts suppliers, a tire vulcanizer and an automobile storage facility, all mixed in with a full complement of traditional carriage and wagon dealers, livery stables and blacksmiths.

Car Sales Gain New Sophistication

What appears to be the first newspaper advertisement in San Antonio for an individual automobile was placed by Frank B. Grice in the *Express* on September 1, 1909, for the American model now referred to as the American Underslung. The car's axles were positioned above the chassis rather than underneath, as is now almost universally the case. This design required oversized wheels, which added to the car's appearance of speed featured in the advertisement.

That speed was now more of an issue than reliability was suggests another indication that the automobile was achieving a certain level of maturity.

Facing page: From 1912 to 1925 the showroom for Franklins was at the southeast corner of Avenue D/ North Alamo Street and Travis Street, a site now occupied by the Federal Building.

Below: By the World War I era the Alamo appeared to be under seige by the automobile. At left, the Clifton George Motor Company's billboard rises from the Ford dealership behind the Alamo. At right, another photographer captured showrooms of the San Antonio Motor Sales Company.

Serving as the shop for the evolving Oldsmobile/Maxwell/Franklin dealership then known as Birdsong & Potchernick was this former home on College Street which connected at the back to the dealer's main building, facing Houston Street. The Majestic Theater now occupies the entire site.

In 1906 the Ford Model N was the most popular automobile in America, though the company did not create an official sales agency in San Antonio for two more years. This coincided with introduction of the Model T, the car that put America and the world on wheels.

At first manufacturers employed central agents in major cities to channel orders for vehicles from others to the factory, thus allowing local agents to maintain only a small inventory. Since agents were being paid by the manufacturer and therefore did not need large amounts of capital to purchase sizable inventories for resale, even smaller communities could have an automobile outlet with only one or two sales per month. On the western edge of Bexar County, the small community of Macdona had two such outlets, one for Overland and another for Ford.

By the 1920s, with roads passable but no reliable means for shipping large numbers of cars to dealerships, dealers could pick up cars at the factory and drive them back for resale. Here Birdsong & Potchernick's Buddy Margale stands beside Seneca Lake near Geneva, New York, "En Route to Sunny San Antonio" from the Franklin factory in Syracuse.

A 1926 Buick parked outside the San Antonio Buick Co. is the backdrop for dealer Henry Bryant, left, who stands in a promotionl photo beside heavyweight boxing champion Jack Dempsey.

Below, a Franklin Pirate Model 147, with air-cooled motor and enclosed running boards, is parked outside Municipal Auditorium in 1930. At bottom, a couple stands for a portrait with their driver and his-and-hers 1925 and 1926 Cadillacs.

In 1907 or 1908, machine shop owner Leo DeHymel became San Antonio's first authorized Ford dealer, the city's longest continuing dealership. DeHymel sold to Charles Cook, who sold in 1910 to Clifton George, also the developer of Alamo Heights.

Behind the Alamo at 720 East Houston Street, George remained the city's principal Ford dealer even after 1916, when Ford began permitting additional dealerships in the same city. In 1925, Ed Herpel, then a Ford dealer in Boerne, joined with George's sales manager, Frank M. Gillespie, to purchase George's firm and rename it Herpel-Gillespie. The dealership later came under Gillespie's sole ownership and was relocated to Broadway and Fourth Street, where it remained for decades until its move north of Loop 410 and purchase by Red McCombs.

San Antonio's oldest dealership operating under basically the same name is Jordan Ford, which James Jordan opened in Boerne in 1919. In 1923 he sold out to Ed Herpel and opened a dealership, first known as Jordan-Ivers Motor Company, at South Alamo and South St. Mary's streets, since moved to IH 35 near Loop 1604. The oldest Texas dealership under the same name is Sames Motor Company of Laredo, which opened in 1910 to sell Fords.

Advice from who would change your flat tires quickly to which battery makes your Ford crank more easily came in the articles and advertisements of *"By George!"*, a magazine published monthly in the World War I era by San Antonio Ford dealer Clifton George.

Employees of the Clifton George Ford dealership gather outside their building in 1915 with the shop foreman, George's son Charles, far right, later a principal in the Nash dealership. In the background is the historic Peter Gallagher home then standing directly behind the Alamo.

Following the damage to their Houston Street location during a flood in October 1913, Birdsong and Potchernick moved into a former livery stable on Avenue D, soon renamed North Alamo Street, and sold only Franklins—"America's Lightest Fine Car." Potchernick, who had opened San Antonio's first automobile parts and accessories store, never played an active role in the auto dealership but concentrated on the sporting goods business. When Birdsong accrued enough capital, he bought Potchernick's share in 1917. He built a new structure at North Alamo and Seventh streets in 1928 as a used car outlet and leased a showroom for Franklins at 712 Broadway. But five years later, as manufacture of Franklins drew to an end during the Depression, Birdsong consolidated his operation to Avenue D and closed altogether in 1936.

In 1918 dealers formed the San Antonio Dealers Association and began sponsoring annual car shows. Four years later there were fifty different models on display for a week at the St. Anthony Hotel. Social clubs and even members of the Army were invited each evening to enjoy the event. Unlike at present-day shows, visitors could buy the vehicles on display. Buick, displayed in the hotel's famous Peacock Alley, was the most popular.

Automobile Races

Automobile races were held on the grounds of the San Antonio International Fair in present-day Riverside Park as early as 1904. Two years later, the legendary racing driver Barney Oldfield broke his own world record at the fairgrounds track by doing a mile in just over one minute–1:07.2. San Antonio fans were even more delighted when the city's Dr. F. J. Fielding defeated Oldfield in a three-mile handicap touring car race.

An even better track in Houston drew the San Antonio Automobile Club's first racing drivers. There the races, organized by the Houston Driving Club, attracted sizable crowds, including a large number of women. The cars were split up into various classes, including some for steam-powered and electric vehicles only. A

This Packard was filled with five spare tires—and a dog—in preparation for the difficulties of a long road trip. It is parked outside San Antonio's new Nash dealership on Travis Street, from where the showroom moved in 1928 to a new building at Broadway and Ninth Street.

San Antonio drivers placed first and second in the five-mile free-for-all race at the Houston Driving Club's track about 1904. In first place at 9.44 minutes—nearly 53 mph—was J. D. Anderson, second from left, who drove a French-built Richard Brazier. Taking second place was Lewis Birdsong, third from left, in an Oldsmobile. At far left is E. J. Russell of Dallas in a one-cylinder Cadillac at far right Houston's George W. Hawkins in an Oldsmobile.

novelty race involved occupants of each car getting out and back into their vehicles after each of six laps around the half-mile oval course.

Lewis Birdsong earned a reputation as a fine driver at the tiller of his relatively small one-cylinder Oldsmobile, in a White steam-powered touring car and also on an Orient motorcycle. Birdsong completed each race he entered in about 1904 but took no first places, though with his respectable number of second places he managed to take home the largest portion of the winnings handed out at the end of the day.

J. D. Anderson, San Antonio's first gasoline-powered car owner, distinguished himself that year in both his Oldsmobile and his French-built Richard Brazier, larger and more powerful than most other cars entered. On the street it would be described as handsome, but when raced it was stripped of all non-essentials, including bodywork and fenders. Anderson won two races outright but was forced to retire due to mechanical problems in a third. Several other cars, including a very fast Cadillac from Dallas, suffered the same fate. Another car was wrecked after it hit a dog on the track.

Other Houston racers included Terrell's Edward Green, who in 1899 was the first to drive a gasoline horseless carriage in Texas. Green only had one leg, but this did not stop him from creditable performances in his 10-horsepower Franklin. Out-of-state participants included at least one car and driver from New York.

In October 1909 the fairgrounds' three-quarters of a mile oval track was upgraded into the San Antonio Speedway, with

W. B. Frasse in his "Green Dragon," a comic class entry in San Antonio auto races in 1913. The entry spoofed legendary driver Barney Oldfield's record-setting vehicle, also known as the Green Dragon.

with wide, well banked turns at both ends. Reported the *New York Times*: "Instead of having a fence around the outside of the track there is to be a sloping wall of earth, so if a driver loses control of his car and the machine runs off the track the grade of the wall will bring it to a stop." The first races were held under the auspices of the San Antonio Automobile Club during the last four days of the fair.

A racing fatality at the fairgrounds track on November 12, 1910 was San Antonio's own "Tobin" DeHymel, already practically a legend at 19 when a wheel broke on his car and he was thrown out. DeHymel, a brother of pioneer San Antonio Ford dealer Leo DeHymel, was a factory race driver for Stoddard-Dayton, manufacturer of sports cars in Dayton, Ohio, in the years when auto companies used race competition for promotional purposes.

DeHymel's real name was Alfred Florence DeHymel. He gained the nickname by which he is known for having been the driver for Bexar County Sheriff John Tobin, presumably a job that rewarded fast driving skills. DeHymel drove in the first auto races at the Indianapolis Motor Speedway in August 1909. He won a twenty-one mile race on the beach at Galveston in 22 minutes 5 seconds. A month before his death, DeHymel had driven in the

Racer Ben Nottingham, right, in his Maxwell in 1910. Below, Jack Specht photographed San Antonio racing star Tobin DeHymel in his Stoddard-Dayton at the San Antonio Speedway in November 1910 shortly before DeHymel's fatal crash.

A Stutz racing car with its driver at Kelly Field in 1923.

sixth running of the Vanderbilt Cup race in New York, then dominated auto races at the Texas State Fairgrounds in Dallas.

Manufacturing Cars in South Central Texas

There were several attempts to build and market cars in San Antonio. In 1898, George H. Lutz managed to make one prototype of a steam-powered car before his company failed. The Commercial Motor Car Company, which also had a Houston address, opened and closed its doors in 1910. The Texas Motor Car Company offered the Tex in 1915 and 1916. The Blumberg Motor Manufacturing Company, which operated in both San Antonio and Orange, Texas, was open for business from 1915 until 1922.

The most successful San Antonio manufacturing venture of the era was the Lone Star Automobile and Truck Company, established in 1919 at 515 Roosevelt Avenue across the tracks from Brackenridge High School under the sponsorship of Piedmont Motor Car Company of Lynchburg, Virginia. Piedmont got real estate and insurance entrepreneur Henry C. Feldman to invest in

"40,000 Miles and Still Running" is the message on the side of this Studebaker that made the trip between Seguin and Detroit. The related Blumberg Motor Manufacturing Company in San Antonio manufactured cars from 1915 to 1922.

The San Antonio showroom for locally manufactured Lone Star automobiles about 1922.

the local company and run it. Using equipment components made by a variety of manufacturers furnished by Piedmont and adding Piedmont's own bodywork design—largely modeled after the contemporary Hudson—Feldman produced the Lone Star automobile in San Antonio.

The Lone Star, representing the transition from open to closed-in cars, featured one model with a permanent hard top with open sides and a rear window of glass rather than clear plastic. Seats in the top models were upholstered in gray leather.

Independent car manufacturers, however, were quickly falling victim to the appeal of annual model changes and the easy

The personal Lone Star of Henry Feldman, head of the Lone Star Automobile and Truck Company that built the cars near Brackenridge High School.

Used car parts were often used to build "new" cars, as did Joseph Bader, top, in Comfort. Kerrville's Harry Dietert, above, built his own car to get to town from his father's ranch.

financing methods of General Motors, which created the General Motors Acceptance Corporation in 1919 and was soon financing nearly 80 percent of its sales. When the Piedmont Motor Car Company failed in 1922, so did the Lone Star Automobile and Truck Company. The only Lone Star known to survive is a four-cylinder open tourer, restored and owned in 2009 by a resident of Port Lavaca.

In 1907 Joseph Bader set up a shop on Main Street in Comfort to rebuild cars from used parts. He experienced enough success to relocate his expanding operation to Kerrville in 1910, but the success of such low-cost vehicles as the Ford Model T ended his line of remanufactured cars a few years later, though he stayed in the repair business for many years.

Individuals were able to build functioning cars for their personal use. The enterprising young Harry Dietert became one of the few vehicle owners in Kerr County when he built two cars to get to high school from his father's ranch outside Kerrville. After building a one-seater, in 1915 he built a two-seater, which he called the Harrymobile; its braking was more a suggestion than a command.

Dietert went on to become an automobile-related metallurgist of note and worked in Detroit for most of his career. The Harrymobile has survived and is prominently displayed in the window of Joe Herring's print shop in Kerrville.

When Joe Sanders returned from World War I to Dittlinger's Flour Mill in New Braunfels, he became the company's chief me-

"I Repair Everything On Wheels" was E. F. Kneupper's motto for his Auto Body Works on San Antonio's River Avenue, now Broadway. So travelers could save on hotel bills, Kneupper would also convert cars into "sleepers." chanic and tended to the growing truck fleet, which carried more of the mill's output than did trains. Using the fleet's worn parts, he built a car for himself, a two-seat roadster he drove until availability of lower-priced cars allowed him to replace with it with a factory-made vehicle.

4. Streetcars, Fire Engines and Trucks

Transportation services in San Antonio got three major boosts within two years—1877 and 1878.

In February 1877, the Galveston, Harrisburg & San Antonio Railway brought the city a rapid and efficient connection with the rest of the world. In July 1878, a modern water system with underground pipes replaced the gravity-driven system of ditches that dated from Spanish times. Long-handled pumps connected to the new water mains made it far easier to fill the far-flung troughs to feed the thirst of horses and mules. The previous month, in June 1878, the San Antonio Street Railway Company began the city's first modern system of public transportation.

Streetcars for San Antonio

The Street Railway Company, run by Augustus Belknap, began with mule-drawn cars on four-foot-wide tracks. The first line ran down the middle of Houston Street west from Alamo Plaza, north to Acequia Street—later Main Avenue—and on to San Pedro Avenue up to the popular San Pedro Park. Soon the line was extended northeast to new the railroad depot on Austin Street.

Belknap's company remained the largest of the four major streetcar companies formed by 1890, when mule-drawn cars were replaced with larger cars powered by overhead electric wires. Now that streetcars no longer had to be light enough for mules to pull them, they could go up slightly higher grades and be larger. Seats were more comfortable, and cars were enclosed for protection from the weather. Speed limits, set for mule-drawn cars at ten miles per hour within two miles of San Fernando Cathedral—and fifteen miles per hour beyond that—were raised to twenty miles per hour for electric cars.

Facing page: A truck and crew at San Antonio Fire Department Station No. 7 at 1414 South St. Mary's St. about 1915.

Below: Two streetcars on the Alamo Heights line appear in this circa 1910 photo, looking northwest across Broadway from opposite the present-day Central Market. At center is the home of Clifton George, whose Ford dealership played a key role in supplying the automobiles that accelerated the suburb's growth.

A streetcar of the San Antonio Traction Company, formed in 1899, pauses on the Fort Sam Houston run.

The San Antonio Street Railway Company's main axis remained Houston Street, which became San Antonio's main thoroughfare. Streetcar transportation helped Houston Street surpass the parallel but narrower Commerce Street, where businessmen had rejected streetcar service for the noise and confusion it would add to that already congested artery. Belknap's line was extended farther west to the International & Great Northern/Missouri Pacific depot, northeast to Fort Sam Houston and adjacent Government Hill and south along South Flores Street to the San Antonio & Aransas Pass Railroad depot.

In 1887 the West End Streetcar Company ran a line out to the new West End development around what is now Woodlawn Lake, with an extension seven years later to the new campus of St. Louis College, now St. Mary's University. Two years later the Alamo Heights Company built a line north out River Avenue/Broadway to the new suburb of Alamo Heights, sparking further development there.

In 1890 the Alamo Electric Street Railroad System built the McCrillis Line from downtown south to the International Fair Grounds and Riverside Park. Shorter lines were the Prospect Hill Street Railroad Company's from the International & Great Northern depot west to Prospect Hill and the Cross Town Railroad's line from the Southern Pacific depot on the eastern edge of town west to San Pedro Avenue.

In an attempt to resolve the difficulties of running overlapping municipal transportation systems without public subsidy, in March 1899 the four major streetcar companies were consolidated into the San Antonio Traction Company. This required re-guaging tracks used by some companies from four feet eight-and-a-half inches to the general local standard width of four feet. The company's charter from the city specified a maximum price per ticket of five cents.

San Antonio's streetcar system soon was responsible for an unexpected situation of national significance. In 1903, the State of Texas mandated that persons under the age of seventeen could purchase tickets on public transportation in the state at half price while they were attending school. The San Antonio Traction Company challenged the state's jurisdiction to grant special immunities based on the Texas constitution and the state's right to violate the company's contract with the city. The U.S. Supreme Court upheld rulings of lower courts that, as agents of the state, municipalities could not make rulings that contradicted state rules but must enforce them, the cited wording of the state constitution notwithstanding.

In 1917 the San Antonio Traction Company was merged with the San Antonio Gas and Electric Company to form the San Antonio Public Service Company. In 1921, a San Antonio streetcar fare issue again ended up in the U.S. Supreme Court, this time over the company's request to raise its fare from five to six cents. The court overruled the city's position that its 1899 contract with the San Antonio Traction Company was valid with the new company. Moreover, the court concluded that by requiring the lower rate the city violated the state constitution by being confiscatory, as the lower rate forced the streetcar company to run at a loss. Streetcar fares went up not to six but to seven cents.

By 1926, ninety miles of streetcar tracks had been laid in San Antonio. But rapid growth of the city was requiring the streetcar company to invest in ongoing extensions of tracks—and to pay for repositioning tracks in the center of streets being widened on one side, to say nothing of also being required to pay one-third of the costs of improving all streets used by streetcars. On top of that, operating costs were rising and passenger revenue was down, as more and more San Antonians drove their own cars.

Automobiles had long been challenging the inflexibility of streetcars. Entrepreneurs were buying automobiles, replacing the seats with benches and then cruising along steetcar routes, enticing waiting customers with a faster ride for a nickel. These cars became known as jitneys, slang for a five-cent piece. In 1915, a national oufit named the 5-Cent Auto Company arrived in San

Workmen on Nolan Street in 1933 pave over tracks of San Antonio's recently closed streetcar lines. The Edward Friedrich home shows in the background.

Packards and Buicks retrofitted as longer vehicles exceeded the ability of streetcars to move large numbers of passengers to specific destinations.

Antonio with cars that could seat twelve passengers, even more in Buicks or Packards that were cut in half to add an additional section. These became especially popular for those attending church or public events, and were also used by companies running tours of the city and missions for visitors.

The San Antonio Traction Company, already finding profitability difficult, complained to the city, which reduced the number of jitneys by imposing a $25 license fee for each one and requiring operators to have drivers licenses and purchase a surety bond.

Motorbuses Replace the Steetcar

In 1923 the San Antonio Public Service Company began experimenting with a more sinister competitor to the streetcar: motor buses built in their own shops using a truck chassis. When Faegol coach buses went into production the next year, the Public Service Company purchased a few. At first the speedier buses were not allowed to compete with streetcars and drop off or pick up

45	45	45	45	45	45	45	45	45	45	45	45
30	30	30	30	30	30	30	30	30	30	30	30
15	15	15	15	15	15	15	15	15	15	15	15
1	2	3	4	5	6	7	8	9	10	11	12

10	**AM**	**PM**	31
9	EMERGENCY	ARMY POST	30
8		BEACON HILL	29
	WOODLAWN	BLANCO	
7	TERRACE	BROADWAY	28
	S. P DEPOT	BROOKS	27
6	SO PRESA	CINCINNATI	
5	SO FLORES	COLLINS GDS.	26
	ST. MARYS	CULEBRA	25
4	SAN PEDRO	DENVER HTS.	
3	RUIZ	EXPOS'TION	24
	RIGSBY	FT. SAM	23
2	PROS. HILL	GUADALUPE	
	NO. FLORES	HIGHLANDS	22
	NOLAN	IOWA	21
DEC.	NOGALITOS	KELLY FIELD	
NOV.	McCULLOUGH	MARTIN	20

0575832

This transfer is good only on next connecting bus after time cancelled to destination punched. If conductor refuses this transfer fare should be paid, and circumstances reported to company's office.

SAN ANTONIO PUBLIC SERVICE CO.

FT. SAM - PROSPECT HILL

Months: OCT. SEP. AUG. JUL. JUN. MAY APR. MAR. FEB. JAN

19 18 17 16 15 14 13 12 11

Five years after beginning motorbus service in 1923, San Antonio's Public Service Company was running 74 buses, closing in on the size of the fleet of streetcars.

passengers along streetcar routes, forcing those living beyond the end of the streetcar line but not going all the way downtown to get off the bus where the streetcar line began and take the streetcar to the interim destination.

Nevertheless, by filling in gaps in service—and by entering Fort Sam Houston, which streetcar lines did not—buses quickly caught on. Subdivisions like Terrell Hills and Olmos Park caught on without benefit of the streetcar, and increased use of the automobile by residents of Alamo Heights caused that streetcar line to be abandoned.

In 1928 a study by the Public Service Company, which was running 135 streetcars and 74 buses daily, simply confirmed that buses were outperforming streetcars in every respect from speed to comfort, and the company began cutting back on streetcar services.

With the Depression came lower ridership and municipal financial hardship. In 1933 the Public Service Company paid the city $250,000 for release from its eight remaining contractual years for streetcar service, and to convert its fleet entirely to buses. The company sold most of the larger streetcars to New York and purchased sixty-eight new buses. Seguin—which got a mule-powered street railway in 1885—had paved over its streetcar tracks in 1915, but San Antonio was the nation's first major city to abandon streetcar service. Corpus Christi followed in 1934, Laredo in 1935, Fort Worth in 1939, Austin and Dallas in 1940, and El Paso in 1947.

As railroad passenger numbers declined, intercity bus ridership in Texas grew from under two million in 1928 to nearly five million the next year. The Texas Motor Transportation Division reported that 969 buses owned by 222 companies drove almost 46 million miles over 31,000 miles of routes with no fatalities.

San Antonio's new bus facility, which opened in 1929 at Martin and Navarro streets, was served by a number of carriers. Among them, Red Ball, which became part of Southland Greyhound, ran three buses daily to Dallas and points in between at 7 a.m., 1 p.m. and 7 p.m., a journey that took eleven hours and cost $7.85. Through connections were available to Chicago for a total

Motorized school buses eliminated the need to walk to rural schools. This converted Model T served as a bus for schoolchildren near Marion, northeast of San Antonio.

of $32.85 and to New York for $53.85. A through ticket to Los Angeles could be purchased for $42.85, some $520 today.

The ability of school buses to transport small numbers of students over long distances within a relatively short time to regional schools with full facilities began leading to the demise of rural one-room schools.

Emergency Vehicles

Emergency services soon found themselves out of the horse-drawn age as well.

Doctors were accustomed to lightweight one-horse wagons with high, narrow wheels capable of carrying just one person and the famous medical bag over any terrain under the worst of conditions and with less strain on the horse. It was easier for the horse to pull a wagon than to have a person's weight on its back, and it was less tiring for the human as well.

As central hospitals developed, they employed similar, covered wagons to bring in patients. These vehicles were given the name ambulance, describing wagons that carried sleeping wagon train guards who had pulled overnight sentry duty. Over time the word has come to refer only to medical vehicles.

The police department operated the first motorized ambulances in San Antonio, but this activity soon passed to funeral homes, though not all funeral homes thought this a good idea; in 1929 Porter Loring quit the business after just a few years. Ambulance

In the early 1920s, Ford manufactured the Model T Doctor's Coupe, above, to take over the function of a doctor's one-horse wagon for house calls.

The term ambulance once described vehicles used by funeral homes, such as this one used by funeral director Henry A. Guerra.

A Fordson tractor rather than horses was used to pull the San Antonio Fire Department's 1898 American La France pumper, now on display at the Texas Transportation Museum.

San Antonio Fire Chief August Goetz and a Dalmation got chaufeurred in this Locomobile.

crews, however, at first were not provided with training on how to care for seriously injured victims. According to Emil Knaus, one of the first fire fighters in the city to be trained as an emergency medical technician, crews had an unsavory reputation for delaying if they thought the patient might die, in order to gain a secondary fee for movement of the corpse.

The San Antonio Police Department's first motorized vehicles were air-cooled Franklins, purchased from Birdsong & Potchernick in 1910. The police soon also began using motorcycles. The business district speed limit was 10 miles per hour, increasing to 18 mph just outside downtown. In more sparsely populated sections of the city the limit was 25 mph, though vehicles approaching from the other direction were required to slow to 15 mph; most roads were still only sixteen feet wide, and the margin of error was limited.

The nation's first electronically linked traffic lights were installed in Houston in 1922. San Antonio got its first set one year later. In the same year the police department retired its last horse and set up a squad to deal with the growing problem of automobile theft.

By 1932 San Antonio police cars could receive messages over the radio from police headquarters, though it would take another three years to gain two-way communication. The department acquired four high-speed patrol cars in 1934. The city's first parking meters were installed in 1936.

Few organizations need more specialized vehicles than the fire service. When the first fire fighting association, the all-volunteer Ben Milam Fire Company, was formed in San Antonio in 1854, members had little more than two-wheeled carts, a few ladders and many buckets.

The first horse-drawn steam pumper arrived in 1868, and by 1877 there were five volunteer organizations. The next year these companies were united as the San Antonio Fire Department, but it remained an all-volunteer force. The new water system enabled installation of fire hydrants, but equipment continued to include

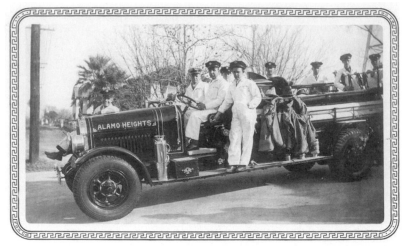

Alamo Heights firemen in 1940 with their ladder truck, manufactured in Buffalo in 1924 and now displayed at the Texas Transportation Museum.

pick up hoses with cylindrical open grills to pump water from rivers and ponds.

The first motorized vehicle acquired by the San Antonio Fire Department was an automobile for the fire chief, probably a gasoline-powered Locomobile, in 1910. About the same time the department began replacing horses with early tractor trucks to pull existing ladder trailers in a crude fifth wheel arrangement. It took a few more years for development of more reliable equipment that allowed power from the engine to be directed to the high-pressure water pumps. By 1917 San Antonio had a number of such vehicles.

In 1924 the new suburban Alamo Heights Fire Department purchased a six-cylinder truck from the Buffalo Fire Truck Company of Buffalo, New York, with mechanical brakes, no synchromesh on its four-speed transmission and no windshield.

Trucks

The introduction in 1919 of heavy-duty low-pressure balloon tires by both Goodyear and Dunlop, and steel wheels, were tremendous boosts for the fledgling trucking industry. The first motorized trucks were crude affairs, most often with solid tires.

This driver in Seguin took early advantage of trucks' flexibility over horsedrawn wagons in hauling freight.

Until tire technology caught up with ever-increasing vehicle weights and speeds, truck drivers were obliged to fix tires all too frequently, usually more often than they filled the trucks with gasoline. Truck drivers had to put up with much discomfort as they steered heavily laden, unwieldy vehicles over unpaved roads. The air cushions provided by balloon tires eased difficulties considerably.

As early as 1917 the largest user of trucks was the beer industry. By 1920, one-fourth of all trucks in Texas were owned by farmers for hauling products to market and returning from town with supplies. Nearly half were based on the Ford Model T, which could be purchased as a chassis-engine combination and then adapted by local companies for non-passenger purposes.

In about 1925 the Clifton George Ford Company showroom featured a Fordson tractor, a Model TT C-cab truck and an enclosed Ford Fordor, with four doors. A similar model with two doors was called—really—a Tudor.

Design of moving trucks, like that of automobiles, had been streamlined by the late 1920s.

In 1917 Ford introduced the TT, or T-Truck, the only significantly different version of the Model T produced by the company during its nineteen-year production run. It had a lengthened and strengthened chassis and a lower ratio rear end to enable the standard twenty-horse power, four-cylinder engine to move heavy loads. This came at the sacrifice of speed, which was reduced to a maximum of 18 miles per hour.

The large variety of Model TT truck cabs and bodies reflects the number of companies involved in constructing them. In 1924 Mission Monument Works purchased a Ford Model TT from the San Antonio Body Company for moving tombstones. The vehicle, in service for decades, has survived, with its now-faded original paint. The post office used TTs for delivering mail. Others were bought as depot hacks by hotels to ferry customers and luggage to and from railroad stations. In 1924 Ford began producing the iconic C cab TT with a simple wooden bed. One purchased by a ranching family in Marfa is now displayed at the Texas Transportation Museum.

In the early twentieth century, some thirty independent companies in Texas manufactured heavy-duty trucks for off-road logging, oil tankers, road construction, buses, fire fighting and military purposes. One of the most successful of these companies had strong ties to San Antonio through Frank A. Winerich, the Woodward Carriage Company president who was seeking to expand his line beyond horse-drawn vehicles. In May 1912 Winerich became the largest investor in the year-old Wichita Falls Car Company. Winerich's efforts to move the company from North Texas to San Antonio were unsuccessful. The company failed in 1932.

Dating from these times is the San Antonio Transportation Association. Formed in 1921, it is the nation's second-oldest trade organization for professionals in trucking and related transportation industries.

5. Driving Beyond San Antonio

As the number of automobiles grew, their owners—typically the most progressive people in the community—began to argue, as had cyclists before them, for improved streets in towns and passable roads to connect the towns. The problem was how to pay for them.

The difficulty of leaving San Antonio for outlying towns was evident by late 1904, when Thomas Conroy invited some friends for a drive to Pleasanton and back in his twenty-four horsepower "Green Man." Various delays caused the party to start back after dark, and the headlights weren't working. A few miles after getting stuck in sand and being dug out by hand, the vehicle ran out of gas. A local farm boy with mules and a wagon returned the men to the city shortly after six the next morning.

Building Roads

Initially, rural road construction funds were raised at the county level from taxation and bonds, with supplemental income from automobile licenses and other fees. This, however, proved insufficient outside large population centers. As a result, there was a great variance in the quality and quantity of roads in Texas. By 1912 only a quarter of the 130,000 miles of roads in the state had

Facing page: Once out of town, a simple mudhole could become a major challenge for early drivers.

Below: This horseless carriage wasn't quite horseless when it came to getting through a long stretch of muddy road.

Grading new roads for automobiles in Texas was accomplished without benefit of motorized vehicles, above, in 1921.

been graded, and only 5,000 miles had a hard surface. The situation would not be adequately financed until the mid-1920s, with introduction of a tax on sale of gasoline.

To build a graded gravel road northwest from San Antonio to Boerne, funds from well-populated Bexar County paid for the project up to the county line. Although since 1904 a change in the Texas constitution had allowed counties to elect to issue road improvement bonds—Bexar County soon issued $500,000 in bonds for San Antonio streets, and another $250,000 three years later—more thinly populated counties had other issues. Kendall County, for one, would not allow higher expenditure on roads in one part of the county at the expense of another area.

Thus to complete the road from the Bexar County line into Boerne, interested individual residents in both counties had to donate funds. As the road did not have a hard surface, it needed to be dragged frequently to fill the deep ruts caused by traffic.

The first attempt to pass federal legislation to provide road improvement funds and create an oversight agency was made in 1911, the same year the idea of a state transportation department in Texas was put forward. Neither campaign was initially success-

Even with a hard surface, rocks presented a regular hazard for the soft treads and inner tubes of early pneumatic tires.

August Herberich, far right, stands beside a more primitive vehicle and its driver, overtaken on the road to Laredo in 1916.

ful, and localities were left to go it alone. By 1915, when the main road through Uvalde was graded and graveled for the first time, San Antonio had 307 miles of hard-surfaced streets, 381 miles of softer-surface Macadam, 36 miles of graded dirt roads and 25 miles of roads surfaced by clay and sand.

The most significant step toward creation of the modern highway system came in 1916 with the passage of the Federal Road Aid Act, the first significant federal legislation to address the need for better roads in the automobile age. In Texas federal money went to creating the sixteen-foot wide macadam Post Road between San Antonio and Austin, which for years was touted as the best road in the state. San Antonio became the headquarters of one of six road department divisions in Texas.

In 1918 the first stretch of highway in Texas to be given an asphalt surface was twenty-five miles between San Antonio and Austin near San Marcos. As many roads outside cities were graded and provided with better drainage, if not with a hard surface, the state speed limit was increased from eighteen to twenty-five miles per hour.

The San Antonio Automobile Club

As automobiles gained a toehold in San Antonio, thirteen owners got together at the Phoenix Athletic Club in October 1903—the same year that the Buick and Ford Motor companies were formed—to organize the San Antonio Automobile Club. Among them were J. D. Anderson—who owned San Antonio's first car and did a little racing in the French-built Richard Brazier racer—and Lewis Birdsong, H. W. Staacke, W. F. Crothers and Fred W. Cook, who was elected president.

For $30,000—the present-day equivalent of $700,000—the group built a stone clubhouse designed by the prestigious architectural firm of Adams & Adams ten miles north of the city on spacious grounds on North Loop Road, now better known as Scenic Loop Road.

The club became the most vocal advocacy group for better roads in the region, leading some drivers living as far away as for-

William and Bertha Schertz are in the rear of a 1912 Franklin Touring Car as it leaves the grounds of the San Antonio Automobile Club on North Loop Road, later known as Scenic Loop, north of San Antonio.

ty-four miles, in Falls City, to apply for non-residential membership status to help support better roads.

The club's first activity was a thirty-mile trip along the recently improved road to Corpus Christi as far as the Medina River, returning via the South Loop. Twelve vehicles gathered at the Crothers & Birdsong store on East Houston Street. Five of the cars were Curved Dash Oldsmobiles, the others a Pope-Toledo, Thomas, Ford, Locomobile steamer, Woods Electric, Haynes-Apperson and Anderson's Richard Brazier. The cars left at 10 a.m. and were back by noon.

The next adventure was to bring election results from outlying areas in the county directly to the editorial offices of the San Antonio *Express*. Some cars had to drive almost forty miles over unimproved roads, but they made the trip in less than two hours. The worst thing that happened was that Birdsong's Oldsmobile lost its muffler, causing it to sound like "a Gatling gun in furious operation." The newspaper was delighted with the results, which it posted on an electric sign outside the building as the evening wore on, much to the delight of the growing crowd. The paper was also receiving national election results by wire service for the first time.

The next outing attracted only three cars—two Oldsmobiles and the Pope-Toledo—for a one-day trip to New Braunfels. The party left from Birdsong & Crothers at 8:05 a.m. and at 11:20 a.m. arrived in New Braunfels, where they had lunch with Mayor

Automobiles gather at the north end of Alamo Plaza, top, before leaving on a run to New Braunfels in 1912. One obstacle was crossing the rockstrewn bed of Cibolo Creek, shown in lower view during an Automobile Club trip to New Braunfels in 1904.

Harry Landa, one of the first residents there to own a car. Along the way the small caravan frightened several teams of horses and had to negotiate immense rocks while crossing the dry bed at Cibolo Creek.

In 1910 the club's president, Robert W. Carr, was elected president of the Texas State Automobile Association. He was succeeded by the secretary, Dr. Richard A. Goeth. In 1907 Goeth had bought a Maxwell from Lewis Birdsong and joined the club, soon becoming chairman of its Good Roads Committee. Upon completion of the road to Boerne, Goeth began advocating its extension to Kerrville. He urged using asphalt as the best material for its surface, having driven on that smooth wonder during a visit to California in 1909. But it would take more than ten years before asphalt became common on other than city streets in Texas.

Finding the Way

Another important role of automobile clubs was development of road maps and directions, for which Dr. Goeth was a leader. Members were exhorted to keep precise logs of all their trips outside the city to record conditions and to help create maps and sets of directions to be published by the national organization. At least two persons were required for this task, one to drive and another to carefully record the times, distances and reference points for turns.

Volunteers chose a well-known starting point. To reach San Antonio from Austin, the mileage starting point in 1909 was the center of the Colorado River bridge. Drivers were instructed to follow the streetcar tracks south for six miles, then at 12.4 miles to ford a small creek at Manchaca Springs and take the right-hand road, where Goeth himself had hung a sign reading "To San Antonio." Upon crossing the railroad tracks at Buda, drivers were

The main road to Corpus Christi presented particular challenges to early automobile drivers. Autos in wet weather sank into the mud and caused deep ruts that, when baked in the sun, forced drivers to straddle them.

to make a right turn at a large store onto Main Street and .2 mile later to take the left-hand road toward Onion Creek, then stay on the left-hand side of the creek. Upon arriving in San Marcos, drivers were to reset the trip odometer to zero for the leg to New Braunfels, where the odometer again was to be reset before continuing on to San Antonio. This itinerary was published in San Antonio and Austin newspapers and by the Automobile Club's national headquarters in Philadelphia, along with a topographical map with rudimentary information about the roads, which were little more than trails.

Volunteers made multiple trips to establish the best routes. However, the signs they placed were often unreliable, as locals along the routes—playful young people or disgruntled farmers who resented the intrusion of noisy and disruptive automobiles on or near their property—often destroyed them or changed the indicated direction. In one case, a farmer near San Marcos, upon learning that his white house was being used as a point of reference in motorist guides, painted it green to confuse the ever-growing number of drivers.

Car enthusiasts continued to stage events to demonstrate the usefulness of automobiles and the need for better roads. One of the best known was the Farm and Ranch Tour organized by *Farm and Ranch Magazine* publisher Frank Holland, who put up a $1,000 prize to encourage participation.

On July 22, 1912, twenty-six cars set out from Dallas across the heart of the state. The next night they stayed in Austin. The following day the remaining twenty-three cars arrived in San Antonio. Drivers and passengers were wined and dined by local dignitaries. Their vehicles remained on Alamo Plaza overnight before the tour headed to Galveston and then back to Dallas.

Civic pride was a useful motivator. August 10, 1913 was declared Good Roads Day by the Bexar County Highway League, one of the largest automobile associations in the state. Headed by David E. Culp, whose enthusiasm led him to membership in some one hundred motoring associations, the call went out to local citizens in San Antonio and Austin and all points in between. Despite the heat of the Texas summer, volunteers were asked to bring their own shovels and other tools to work on the highway and demonstrate support for better roads.

The Old Spanish Trail Connects San Antonio

At a time when there were not yet one hundred miles of continuously paved highways in all of Texas, in 1915 a grand vision arose for a highway paved continuously from the Atlantic to the Pacific—from St. Augustine, Florida, to Los Angeles, California. This was a distance of 2,817 miles, roughly the route of present-day IH 10.

As a marketing tool the route was given the picturesque name the Old Spanish Trail, much as the first northern transcontinental route, from New York to San Francisco, had been designated the Lincoln Highway when it was proposed in 1912.

Cities, counties and individuals, however, would have to fund the construction, one payoff being the anticipated large volume of revenue from tourists. Travelers wishing to see more of the country could buy Old Spanish Trail maps and guides and follow OST route markers attached to lamp posts within towns and, in the country, painted on trees, telephone poles and fence posts.

Although the route was initially planned to go through Dallas and Fort Worth, a large delegation from San Antonio packed the Old Spanish Trail conference in Houston in 1919 and rectified the situation. San Antonio assumed leadership of the OST within Texas, and a headquarters opened at the Gunter Hotel under the directorship of Harral Ayers.

A route was surveyed paralleling the Southern Pacific Railroad, which could provide easy transportation for road materials and equipment along the way. The road deviated from the railroad if counties offered greater financial support. Gonzales County did

Efforts to complete a southern transcontinental highway that approximately parallels today's IH 10 were headquartered in the Gunter Hotel in San Antonio, midway along the route.

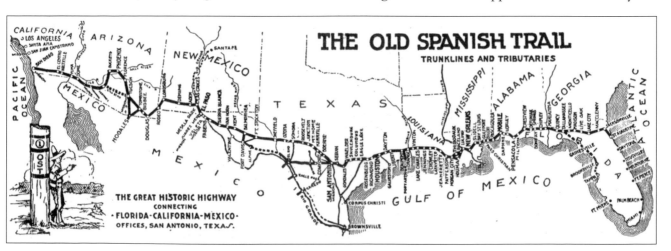

A Zero Milestone marker for drivers to set their odometers before starting out on the Old Spanish Trail Highway was dedicated in front of San Antonio's Bexar County Courthouse in 1924 by Governor Pat Neff.

just that, so the Old Spanish Trail swung south between Flatonia and Seguin, avoiding Luling at the southern tip of the less generous Caldwell County. An alternative OST tourist route, financed with contributions from the area, went through Bandera, where the Old Spanish Trail Restaurant, opened in 1921, is one of the last remaining originally named eating establishments along the route.

The Old Spanish Trail got a major boost with new federal funding when Harral Ayres successfully lobbied for its entire length to be designated part of the military road network. This was to prevent the gridlock experienced during World War I, when the government was forced to take over the tangled railroad system, then backed up only by a network of unimproved roads quickly ruined by the solid tires of long truck convoys.

In March 1924 Texas Governor Pat Neff Neff dedicated the OST zero milestone outside the Bexar County Court House. There drivers could reset their perhaps unreliable odometers for the next leg of the journey. Drivers ceremoniously marking the route's completion were greeted with a grand dinner at the Gunter Hotel as they headed east from Los Angeles through San Antonio on April 4, 1929.

San Antonio was a significant stopping point on a number of major north-south highways as well. One of the first was the Glacier to Gulf Motorway from Calgary in Canada through Montana, Wyoming and New Mexico to Brownsville. Another was the King of Trails, which ran almost directly south from Winnipeg through Minnesota and Iowa to Oklahoma and on through Dallas, Waco and Austin before joining the Glacier Highway route to Brownsville. The Meridian Highway also began in Winnipeg but ran through the Dakotas and Kansas to San Antonio and on to Laredo.

The early era of efforts by enthusiasts and amateurs was over. A state gasoline tax, passed in 1924, finally provided sufficient

Noted Texas rancher John G. Kenedy poses with his new Franklin sedan outside his town home in Corpus Christi in 1927.

funds to build an adequate system of continuously paved highways within Texas. The road from San Antonio to Austin was widened from sixteen to forty feet, sharp curves were eliminated and the road was straightened, shortening its length by eight miles. The Texas Department of Transportation had grown to sixteen divisions, employing hundreds of engineers and road gangs. More growth was to come, as the automobile industry had grown to become the nation's largest.

Yet travel across the region was still a hit-or-miss affair. As late as 1929 a San Antonio guidebook recommended that persons should not travel by road outside the city if it had rained recently, was raining or looked as though it might. The large number of pictures of cars stuck axle-deep in endless mud attests to the wisdom of this advice. The road to Corpus Christi seems to have been particularly bad, running as it did through some less affluent counties. Along the Gulf coast the road surface consisted of crushed seashells.

Even the vaunted Old Spanish Trail was not much better. From San Antonio through the Hill Country the road may technically have been improved, but in many cases this meant only that it had been graded and provided with ditches for drainage. Numerous sections remained unpaved.

Wheels in Smaller Towns

Towns around San Antonio had their own challenges adapting to the automobile. Two years after the local doctor brought the first automobile to Comfort—a two-cylinder Maxwell, in 1906—the ford over the Guadalupe River was replaced with a low wooden bridge, which soon proved no match for high water. A more substantial concrete bridge two feet above the water was built in 1914 and survives. Following its completion, however, little more was done to improve roads in the area for almost twenty years.

A concrete bridge built slightly above the waters of the Guadalupe River at Comfort in 1914 is still in use.

Mechanized transport developed in towns around San Antonio in a parallel fashion. Uvalde had its own streetcar system, left. A Model T joins horsedrawn vehicles at a mercantile establishment in Devine, center. Three Paterson 30s and a Buick, at bottom, line up around a park in Kerrville.

The Model T that carried the mail between Bandera and Tarpley is parked, with its spare tire, outside the *Frontier Times* building in Bandera.

The unpaved streets of Comfort were still dragged every day until federal Depression-era programs began.

In the larger town of New Braunfels to the east, the VFW post under the leadership of Joe Sanders began placing handmade signs along country roads and at intersections for the benefit of the growing number of motorists. In 1919 Comal County posted speed signs in and around New Braunfels and hired two motorcycle officers to enforce the 18 miles per hour speed limit on the road between San Antonio and Austin.

With growing popularity of the automobile, dealerships also opened in smaller towns. The first dealership in New Braunfels, the Gerlich Auto Company, opened in 1912, selling Fords. The first agency in Kerrville was for the Buick, soon followed by a Brush agency. Emergency services gradually adopted motorized vehicles, as with the ladder truck upgraded from horsepower to tractor power by the Wichita Falls Truck Company for Seguin's volunteer fire department in 1927.

Arrival of new automobiles like this Franklin drew crowds in small towns like Pettus, toward Corpus Christi.

Numerous cross-country bus lines developed throughout Texas like Painter, one of its vehicles shown in Uvalde in about 1930.

Truck lines springing up to serve outlying areas included Lynn Hensley's, which ran two medium-duty Chevrolet trucks daily between San Antonio and points northeast.

Regional freight hauling was initially dominated by small companies, often one-person, one-vehicle operations. Most small towns had at least one such firm. In Marion, between Seguin and San Antonio, it was run by Lynn Hensley. His operation consisted of two medium-duty Chevrolet bobtails, a truck with a longer bed supported by four rear wheels on a single axle.

In Cotulla, halfway between San Antonio and Laredo, motorized freight hauling was initially done by Roy Gilbert. His father, a dairy farmer, had built a rough-looking truck from old parts in the early 1920s to haul his produce to San Antonio. Friends and neighbors asked him to take things, too. Gilbert found he was making as much money hauling goods as he was farming, so he decided to get into the business full time. In 1930 his son acquired a second truck and formed Gilbert Truck Lines, which expanded rapidly to other towns.

Even though improved roads outside city limits were a long way off, some enterprising individuals began to offer transportation between towns as well. One of the first scheduled services in Texas was begun in 1912 by Josh Merritt, who used a 1906 Packard converted to seat seven passengers between San Marcos—on the Missouri Pacific Railroad—and Luling, on the Southern Pacific. Merritt did well enough that he was able to expand his service to Austin and Gonzales. One of the first bus routes out of San Antonio was started in 1922 by Louis Creamer to take workers to the oil fields in Eastland.

At first there were no rules for bus operations. Providers had to register their vehicles but had no obligations regarding insurance or surety bonds. Cutthroat rivalries developed. In one case, Kerrville residents enjoyed free rides for several weeks as two competitors tried to force each other out of business. Serious contenders attempting to operate larger and safer buses were thwarted as competitors with old cars emerged to undercut their fares.

In 1927 such cars and larger buses were providing service between Kerrville and San Antonio ten times daily in each direction, while Southern Pacific struggled to provide a single passenger train each day. Larger bus operators formed a trade group to lobby for strict regulations, and that year the state enacted the Motor Bus Law, six years before similar federal legislation was passed. The surviving line on the Kerrville–San Antonio route is the Kerrville Bus Company, begun in 1925 by Hal and Charlie Peterson with two converted Buicks.

Epilogue

Reminders of the early era of automobiles remain scattered incognito throughout San Antonio. The galleries and offices of ArtPace, above, occupy a renovated Hudson dealership at 445 North Main Avenue. The Art Deco landmark Packard dealership building at 1123 North Main Avenue has been restored, and the Cadillac dealership at Dallas Street and Lexington Avenue on Crockett Park has been renovated as a condomninium complex known as Cadillac Lofts.

After World War II, automobiles in San Antonio reached such a point that Fortune magazine, in 1957, found that among all major cities in the nation, San Antonio had the highest proportion of residents using personal vehicles to access the center of the city. San Antonio had 78 percent, Los Angeles 66 percent and New York 17 percent. Los Angeles had the highest proportion of residents using automobiles for all urban travel—95 percent.

Public transportation was then in the hands of the privately held San Antonio Transit Company, created in 1941 when American Light and Traction, parent company of the San Antonio Public Service Company, was forced by an anti-trust decision to divest many of its components.

In San Antonio, the electrical generation component went to the city, which ran it as City Public Service. A group of Texas investors took over the transportation division and moved it into the 1929 landmark Smith-Young Tower, which then became known as the Transit Tower until the structure was taken over by an insurance company and got its present name, the Tower Life Building.

From its offices in the Transit Tower, the company dealt with a passenger load vastly increased by incoming wartime military personnel, from twenty-two million riders in 1939 to thirty-six million in 1942. Since manufacture of buses was suspended during the war, the Transit Company had to scrounge used buses from private companies, the Army and even bring retired buses back into service, including some of the Faegols purchased in 1924. Mechanics trying to maintain these buses were not helped by the wartime slowdown in road maintenance, which increased wear and tear on all vehicles.

In 1959 Transit Company investors were bought out by the City of San Antonio, which created the San Antonio Transit System and eventually, in 1977, the VIA Metropolitan Transit Authority. In five years VIA built ridership from 20 million back close to the World War II level, with 34.5 million riders by 1981. VIA was named North America's best transit system in 1990 and the second most cost-effective public transportation service in 1994. In 2000 it reintroduced buses powered by propane, cutting costs and reducing emissions.

During the Depression, bicycle use increased as an alternative to walking or paying seven cents to ride the streetcar or bus. Bicycle racks outside schools were full. Grocery stores used bikes with

In 1958, Red McCombs, right, joined Austin Hemphill in the descendant of San Antonio's longest surviving auto dealership, established in 1907/08, and turned it into the sixth-largest auto conglomerate in the United States.

Two Toyota Tundras at the San Antonio plant that opened in 2006 with more than 2,000 employees.

small front wheels to accommodate a large basket for local deliveries. Ice cream vendors used a tricycle arrangement to carry their wares in a large insulated ice box over the front wheels. Schoolboys used bicycles to deliver newspapers.

The oil crisis of the early 1970s brought about a new interest in bicycling. The San Antonio Wheelmen gained some seventy members within a year of its birth in 1971. The venerable Charles A. James Bicycle Co. was still suplying the local market, and a dozen new specialty bike stores opened. Bicycle lanes were designated on city streets, bicycle racks were installed on city buses, police officers began downtown bike patrols—in 1990—and group rides were planned by an organization named Chain Reaction. Bike rides to benefit charities became common. Motors played their role on two-wheelers. By 2000 more motorcycles than heavy-duty trucks were registered in Texas, by a score of 187,000 to 155,000.

By the end of the Depression, the large number of independent automobile manufacturers had shrunk to the Big Three—General Motors, Ford and Chrysler—and the Small Five—Hudson, Nash, Studebaker, Packard and Willys-Overland. One effort to add diversity to a model line was Ford's introduction of the short-lived Edsel in 1957. The Winerich Motor Company held San Antonio's Edsel franchise.

A future San Antonio automobile sales magnate, B. J. "Red" McCombs, got the Edsel franchise for Corpus Christi and became the nation's top-selling—and youngest—Edsel dealer, one of the few to make a profit. In 1958 McCombs joined San Antonio Ford dealer Austin Hemphill, later bought him out and eventually owned the sixth-largest auto conglomerate in the United States, with more than fifty dealerships.

As foreign manufacturers moved some manufacturing to the United States, San Antonio suddenly found itself with a major assembly plant. A rural site in southern Bexar County once planned to be submerged as a reservoir was found by Toyota to be ideally situated with rail links and proximity to a growing market in both Texas and Mexico for such full-size pickup trucks as the Ford F150, Chevrolet Silverado and Dodge Ram. San Antonio's plant would initially produce the competing new Toyota Tundra.

Four years later, on November 17, 2006, Toyota opened its $50 million San Antonio plant. It had more than 2,000 employees and the capacity to produce 200,000 trucks annually. More than a dozen independent suppliers were building facilities nearby, helping San Antonio do its part to keep the world on wheels.

San Antonio Road Rules, 1910

An Ordinance Regulating Traffic on the Streets, Plazas and Public Places of the City

Be it ordained by the City Council of the City of San Antonio:

That the following rules and regulations are hereby established for the regulation of traffic on the streets, plazas and public places of the City of San Antonio and the government of the owners, operators, drivers, or persons in charge of carts, drays, wagons, hacks, carriages, omnibuses, bicycles, motor cycles, automobiles or other vehicles.

SECTION I

1. Vehicles going in opposite directions shall pass each other on the right.

2. All vehicles shall keep close to the curb on the right, provided that a vehicles overtaking another shall go to the left of the overtaken vehicle in passing, but it shall not turn out to the left unless there is a clear way of at least one hundred feet ahead on the left, free.

3. The driver of any vehicle shall stop upon a signal from any peace officer.

4. A vehicle shall not turn to the left into another street without passing to the right of and beyond the center of such or the next intersecting street as the case may be, before turning, and vehicles turning to the right into another street shall keep close to the curb on the right.

5. A vehicle crossing from one side of a street to the other shall do so by turning about to the left so as to head in the direction of traffic on that side of the street.

6. When an automobile, other motor vehicle or any other character of vehicle whatsoever approaches a street car which has stopped for the purpose or permitting persons to alight therefrom or get upon said street car, the said automobile, motor vehicle or other vehicle shall immediately slow down and pass said street car slowly and in a very cautious manner; and in turning any corner where cars are stationary for the purpose of receiving or discharging passengers, no such automobile, motor vehicle or other vehicle shall travel at any speed that may endanger person alighting from or desirous of entering said street car, which shall be considered reckless driving, and a violation of this ordinance.

7. It shall be unlawful for any person to drive or propel any vehicle upon any sidewalk, or to allow any vehicle driven or propelled by him or her to stand upon any sidewalk.

8. It shall be unlawful for any person in charge of any horse or other domestic animal to tie or hitch such horse or other animal to any fire

> *"It shall be unlawful for any person to drive or propel any vehicle upon any sidewalk."*

plug, lamp-post, telegraph, telephone or fire alarm post or United States mail box post.

9. It shall be unlawful for any person in charge of any vehicle or domestic animal to allow said vehicle or domestic animal to allow said vehicle to remain standing or hitch or tie such animal within thirty feet of any intersecting street within the limit of one mile from the cupola of San Fernando Cathedral.

10. Every driver of a vehicle shall before slowing or stopping, give a signal to those behind by the voice or the raising of a hand.

11. Before backing a vehicle to unload or load, ample warning shall be given by voice or by the raising of the hand, so as to prevent injury to those behind.

12. No vehicle shall stop with its left side to the curb.

13. No vehicle shall be driven through a procession, nor shall any vehicle remain on any street in such manner as to interfere with the passage of such procession.

14. No vehicle shall be backed up to the curb to load or unload on Commerce or Houston streets, between Alamo and North Flores streets between the hours of 8 a.m. and 7 p.m.

15. No vehicle shall remain standing on Houston or Commerce streets, between Alamo and North Flores streets between the hours of 8 a.m. and 7 p.m. for a longer period than 20 minutes.

16. No vehicle shall stop at any street crossing in such a manner as to obstruct free passage over such crossing.

17. No vehicle shall stop or remain standing on any street a greater distance than 12 inches from the curb, nor shall any vehicle stop or remain on any street in such a way as to obstruct free passage of traffic thereon.

18. No vehicle shall travel the streets within a limit of one mile from the cupola of San Fernando Cathedral at a greater speed than eight miles per hour, and at no greater speed than fifteen miles per hour within the city limits outside of the first mile limit; provided, however that no vehicle shall be driven in a careless or reckless manner at any rate of speed, regardless of whether such rate comes within the above limit or not.

19. No vehicle shall cross any street or bridge or make any turn at street intersections at a greater speed than one half the legal speed rate upon such street, nor in a careless or reckless manner at any rate of speed. Provided that no person shall ride or drive any animal whether attached to a vehicle or not, over any bridge across the San Antonio River or San Pedro Creek, at a faster gait than a walk, nor shall any person drive, lead or ride any animal or vehicle over any foot bridge within the city.

20. No person shall operate, drive or propel any automobile or other motor vehicle in the streets of this City unless he shall have been first duly examined by the City Physician and an examiner to be appointed by His Honor the Mayor, and found fully competent mentally and physically by said examiners, and certificate thereof furnished by said examiners to the City Engineer, who shall thereupon issue to said applicant a non-transferable license or permit, for which examination the applicant shall pay to said examiner a fee of Two Dollars for the use of the City. Said permit shall be carried on the person of said applicant while driving or propelling any automobile or other motor vehicle and be exhibited on demand of any peace officer.

"No person shall operate, drive or propel any automobile or other motor vehicle in the streets of this City unless he shall have been first duly examined by the City Physician and an examiner to be appointed by His Honor the Mayor."

21. The owner of any automobile shall, before operating same or permitting the same to be operated, exhibit to the City Engineer, his certificate or registration from the County Clerk, and register with the City Engineer his name and residence together with a description of the vehicle so owned, and the City Engineer shall enter such name, residence, description and number of his certificate of registration in a record kept for that purpose, and to furnish to said owner said number, which shall be composed of figures not less than six inches in height, and of white material as he may designate, for which number said owner shall pay to the City Engineer, for the use of the City, the sum of Two Dollars, and which number shall be placed or cause to be placed by the owner of such vehicle, on the rear of his vehicle and be rigidly fastened to the body in such manner that when the rear lights of such vehicle are lit, the said number shall be plainly discernable at a distance of not less than fifty feet. The said figures shall at all times be kept clean so that the same may be easily recognized, and shall not at any time be concealed or covered up, but shall be kept in plain sight.

22. The owner of any motor vehicle other than an automobile shall, before operating same, apply to the City Engineer for a permit and make application therefor, stating his name and residence together with a description of the vehicle so owned, and the City Engineer shall enter such name, residence, description and number of permit, if granted, in a record kept for that purpose, and shall award to said owner a special number, corresponding with the number of his permit, for which said owner shall pay to said City Engineer, for the use of the city, the sum of One Dollar, and which number shall be placed or cause to be placed on the rear of his vehicle and rigidly fastened thereto, in such a manner as to be easily discernable at a distance of not less than 30 feet. The said number shall be composed of such figures, not less than three inches in height, and of such material and color as may be selected by the City Engineer, and shall at all times be kept bright and plainly to be seen, and shall never be concealed or covered up.

23. It shall be unlawful for any person to drive or operate an automobile or other motor vehicle on the streets of this city without first registering under oath with the City Engineer in a suitable record kept for that purpose his or her name, age, address, occupation, together with a statement as to the condition of his or her sight and hearing in addition to the requirements of the preceding paragraphs. It shall then be the duty of the City Engineer to furnish everybody registered, who has complied with all the provisions of this ordinance, a non-transferable certificate of registration, for which he shall collect, for the use of the City, a fee of twenty-five cents. Said certificate shall be good until the first day of June following the date thereof. Not more than one certificate shall be issued to any persons within one fiscal year. Provided that the conviction of any person holding such certificate, permit or license, for the third time within twelve months, of any provision of this ordinance, shall work an immediate cancellation of such certificate, permit or license; and such person shall not be allowed to obtain or be entitled to another permit for a period of six months thereafter.

24. The sale or transfer of a licensed automobile or of a licensed vehicle shall be recorded by the parties making such sale or transfer, in

> *"The conviction of any person holding such certificate, permit or license, for the third time within twelve months, of any provision of this ordinance, shall work an immediate cancellation of such certificate, permit or license."*

the office of the City Engineer, in a record kept for that purpose, with forty-eight hours after such sale or transfer has been consummated, and pay a fee of twenty-five cents therefore, to the City Engineer, for the use of the City; and failure to do which shall render all of such parties guilty of a violation of this ordinance.

25. Every automobile shall between one hour after sunset and one hour before sunrise carry two lights, one on each side, of at least four candle power, to be set in front of a reflector, and one light near the left rear corner of the body of such vehicle, which latter light shall throw a white light on the number of such vehicle and a red light to the rear; every bicycle or motor cycle shall carry a white light in front of not less than two candle power, and every other vehicle shall carry one or more white lights in front or on sides so as to be plainly visible not less than fifty feet.

26. Any person driving or operating an automobile, motor cycle, or other vehicle shall at the request of or in response to a signal by a person riding or driving a horse or horses, or other domestic animals which show signs of fright, cause such vehicle or machine to come to a standstill as quickly as possible, and to remain stationary long enough to allow such animal or animals to pass.

27. No person shall run or drive any motor car or other motor vehicle upon or over the public streets which has an unusually loud exhaust or otherwise makes an unusually loud, uncommon or unnecessary noise.

28. No person shall operate, or cause to be operated, an automobile or motor vehicle upon any of the streets, alleys or public grounds of the City of San Antonio without complying with the provisions herein, provided that the provision of the ordinance relating to the registration and number of such automobile or motor vehicle shall not apply to non-resident visitors for a period of five consecutive days.

SECTION II

1. No person shall engage in any conduct upon any avenue, street or driveway, which shall be likely to frighten horses, injure passengers or embarrass the passage of vehicles thereon.

2. No person not the owner or the one in charge shall, except with the permission of such owner or one in charge, enter or meddle with or in any way handle any automobile or motor car or other vehicle left on the streets, alleys or plazas of the City.

3. It shall be unlawful for any pedestrian to cross or stand upon any street in such way as to interfere with the traffic on that street.

SECTION III

Any person violating any of the provisions of this ordinance shall be deemed guilty of a misdemeanor and upon conviction therefore shall be fined in any sum not less than Five Dollars nor more than One Hundred Dollars for each offense, and every day such violation shall constitute a separate offense, and in addition the license or permit shall be annulled as provided in Subdivision 23 of Section 1 hereof.

Passed and approved February 7, A.D. 1910

BRYAN CALLAGHAN, Mayor

"No person shall engage in any conduct upon any avenue, street or driveway, which shall be likely to frighten horses, injure passengers or embarrass the passage of vehicles thereon."

San Antonio Automobile Dealers, 1922

Alberts Motor Sales Co., 211 S. Flores St.

Baker Motor Co., 151–25 Main Ave.

Bexar Motor Sales Co., 516 Main Ave.

Birdsong & Potchernik, 124 Ave. D; *Franklin*

Blumberg Motor Manufacturing Co., 633 N. Mesquite St.

Buick Motor Co., 302–04 Avenue C; *Buick*

Burton–Lary Motors Co., 403 Ave. C; *Hupmobile, Chandler*

Chaddick Auto Co., 103 San Pedro Ave.

Citizens Auto Co., E. Romana St. at Oakland St.; *Packard*

Crockett Auto Co., 101 Oakland St.; *Hudson, Essex*

Davies Motor Co., 721–23 Navarro St.; *Stephens Salient Six*

Dorman & Voss, 1111 W. Houston St.

Elite Auto Sales Co., 102–08 Garden St.

Clifton George Motor Co., 720 E. Houston St.; *Ford, Lincoln*

H. R. Grote, 320 Navarro St.

Guarantee Motor Car Co., E. Romana St. at Augusta St.; *Maxwell, Chalmers*

Jordan & Columbia Autos, 404 Soledad St.

LaFayette, Deutsch Co., 443–45 Main Ave.; *Lafayette*

Morgan–Woodward Auto Co., 234 S. Flores St.; *Ford*

Jack W. Neal Auto Co., 321–29 S. Flores St.; *Chevrolet*

Orsinger Motor Sales Co., 443–45 Main Ave.

San Antonio Buick Co., 446–56 Main Ave.; *Buick*

San Antonio Cadillac Co., 411–17 N. Main Ave. & 410–16 N. Flores St.; *Cadillac*

San Antonio Motor Co., 310 W. Travis St.

San Antonio Oakland Co., 237–39 E. Romana St.

San Antonio Roamer Co., 445 Main Ave.; *Roamer*

South Texas Motors Co., 1316–18 Grayson St.; *Elcar, Stanley Steamer*

Willys Saint Claire Co., 744 E. Houston St.

Wilson–Fielder Motor Co., 430 Main Ave.

Winerich Motor Sales Co., 301–05 Ave. C; *Studebaker*

Wroten–Hundley Motor Co., Ave. E at Eighth St.; *Dodge*

Yantis–Herpel Motor Co., 317–21 Ave. C; *Ford*

Listen Zander Motor Co., 602–04 Ave. D

Source: *Appler's General Directory and Household Directory of Greater San Antonio*, 1922–1923

Automobile Manufacturers in Texas

Arlington

    1911   Little Motor Kar Co. (also Dallas); *Little Kar*

    1954–   General Motors; *Chevrolet, GMC, Suburban, Tahoe*

Austin

    1968–?   Bushmaster Co.; Bushmaster

Cleburne

    1911–14 Cleburne Motor Car Manufacturing Co.; *Luck* (truck), *Luck Utility, Cleburne*

    1918–22 Texas Motor Car Association (also Fort Worth); *Texan*

Comanche

    1915   Holden Three Wheeler Co.; *Holden Three Wheeler*

Dallas

    1909–70 Ford Motor Co.; *Ford* cars and trucks

    1920   Texas Truck and Tractor Company; *Texas*

    1920–22 Wharton Motors Co. (also Kansas City, MO); *Wharton*

    1922   Little Motor Kar Co. (also Arlington); *Texmobile*

    1964–65 Vanguard Motors Corp.; *Vetta Ventura*

Fort Worth

    1918   Bridges Motor Car and Rubber Co.; *Bridges*

    1918–22 Texas Motor Car Association (also Cleburne); *Texan*, car and truck

    1922   McGill Motor Car Co.; *McGill*

Garland

    1946–47 Southern Aircraft; *Roadable*

Goose Creek

    1946   Frank Inman; *Inman*

Grand Prairie

    1920–22 Little Motor Car Co.; *Little Car*

Houston

    1905–06 Hawkins Automobile and Gas Engine Co.; *Hawkins*

    1908–10 Southern Motor Car Co.; *Dixie Junior, Dixie Tourist*

    1920–24 Southern Motors Co.; *Southern Six, Ranger* truck

Kermit

    1968   VWC Specialty Co.; *Paisano Dune Buggy*

Orange

    1915–22 Blumberg Motor Car Co. (also San Antonio); *Blumberg*

San Antonio

    1898   George H. Lutz; *Lutz* (steam-powered)
    1910   Commercial Motor Car Co. (also Houston); *San Antonio*
    1915–16 Texas Motor Car Co.; *Tex*
    1915–22 Blumberg Motor Manufacturing Co. (also Orange);
                Blumberg
    1917–22 Lone Star Motor Car Company; *Lone Star*
    1920–21 Lone Star Truck and Tractor Association; *Lone Star* truck
    1921   Robertson Co.; *Robertson*
    2006–   Toyota; *Tundra* pickup

Waco

    1914–16 Hall Cyclecar Manufacturing Co.; *Hall Cyclecar*

Wichita Falls

    1911–32 Wichita Falls Motor Co.; *Wichita* heavy-duty truck,
                Wichita Combination Car

Index